"Annie Meehan is a blessed exception. She represents the unexpected, the unpredictable and celebrated survivors of impossible odds. In this book she is a guide—a trusted guide, because she has walked a most difficult path throughout her life. She knows where she's been, knows where she is, and she knows where she is going. Her life has been hardened by troubles that would have ended most of us. And yet there is kindness and understanding in her words. Reading *Be the Exception*, you will be inspired and encouraged by this book. Annie Meehan is a guide in a baffling and often frightening journey where we have felt lost and afraid. She takes our hand, peers into the dark path ahead, and says, 'You can make it.' You believe her—because she did."

—Don Shelby, Emmy Award-winning journalist and former anchor of WCCO-TV

"We all had visions of what we wanted to be when we grew up. It was always based on profession and not on how we operate as people. Reading *Be the Exception* will help us rethink who we want to be when we grow up."

—Walter Bond, speaker, television host, and former NBA player

"Here's a quick read to challenge you to disrupt your normal flow or negative brain patterns and even a negative history of dysfunction and pain! Annie tells vignettes of her story and releases energy and examples and exercises to challenge you to re-tell your story as well. Live the exceptional choice!"

—Nancy Lee Gauche, pastor

Laura,
Wishing you joy on your
journey - Live by Choice
Not Chance or Circumstance

Be the Exception!

Authentically
Annie

Be The
Exception

Your 7 Steps to Transformation

Annie Meehan

ISBN 978-1-63489-900-0
eISBN 978-1-63489-901-7

Library of Congress Catalog Number: 2015960989
Printed in the United States of America
Second Printing: 2017
20   19   18   17   5   4   3   2

Cover design by Theresa French

Wise Ink Creative Publishing
837 Glenwood Ave.
Minneapolis, MN 55405
www.wiseinkpub.com

To order, visit www.itascabooks.com or call 1-800-901-3480.
Reseller discounts available.

Dedication

This book is in memory of my brother, Paul, and my friend Debbie. Their much-too-early deaths have inspired me to have courage to be different, compassionate, and kind to all I encounter.

I also want to honor my birth daughter whose existence gave my life more purpose. My hope is that this story might be a blessing to the sacrifice of all birthmothers everywhere.

To my mother, with love; through our struggles you showed me examples of how to work hard, never give up, and develop a strong faith.

To my husband, Greg, and my wonderful children; I love you. Thank you for showing me what home means.

Contents

"ALL SERIOUS DARING STARTS FROM WITHIN."
—JOAN BAEZ

Introduction

"WE DO NOT NEED MAGIC TO CHANGE
THE WORLD, WE CARRY ALL THE POWER WE NEED
INSIDE OURSELVES ALREADY: WE HAVE THE
POWER TO IMAGINE BETTER."
—J.K. ROWLING

By the time I was eighteen, I had lived in eighty-three different locations: homes, friends' couches, basements, cars, group homes, and safe houses. I was the middle of seven kids and invisible to my siblings and my parents. I never really felt comfortable, and I was always searching for a place to call home, a place where I could feel stable and secure.

Packing up to go to a soccer game is a routine for some families. My family's norm was to pack up the station wagon and move on to the next place. Our move in 1970 was a big one: with seven people in the car, we drove across the country from California to Champaign, Illinois to go live in a red house. My pregnant mom drove the entire distance since my father never learned to drive. We were heading east so that he could go to college—an endeavor that didn't last longer than our next move. We slept at rest stops and ate peanut butter sandwiches for every meal. As a small child, moving was an adventure, with big boxes to play in and new neighborhoods to discover and friends to meet.

But what the adventure was hiding was shame, anger, and hurt. We were constantly surrounded by angry parents, chaos, and tension in the household. Dad wasn't the type to look too hard for a job, and Mom was exhausted emotionally and physically worn down. She did all the grocery shopping, cooking, and cleaning in addition to working full time. She even drove herself to the hospital for the seven deliveries and three miscarriages that she underwent in a ten-year span. It was a happy day for my mom when her oldest daughter was able to help out by fetching a diaper.

My mother was relaxed, beautiful, well-dressed, and fun before she had children. She was employed by a foreign embassy; she travelled the world; she had money, friends, and a life. When she met my dad, her life changed drastically. She was thirty-five years old when she married him. She was already pregnant, and her wedding gown was red, laced with shame.

In her younger years, she'd had the luxury of only taking care of herself; but once she had kids, her life was filled with tasks. She woke up every day with everyone else's needs coming before her own. She was filled with resentment and bitterness, sorrow and regret, and the inability to forgive herself for mistakes she'd made. Because of the stress and hardships, my mother became a hoarder, squirreling away paper, clothing, and containers until we couldn't even walk through some rooms.

In the red house in Champaign, I shared a bed with my three sisters. It was there I realized that it wasn't just covers piled on top of me: I was suffocating, smothered by a household of secrets, mental illness, and dysfunction.

During my childhood, my six siblings and I rarely had enough to eat. Oftentimes, we asked the neighbors to feed us, but other times, we had to jump in dumpsters to get food after stores had thrown it out. Back then, food shelves weren't as accessible as they are today, and a family as large as ours went through a lot of food.

I know now people call what we did *dumpster diving*, but back then, we called it dinner. For us kids, it was a game—we didn't quite understand why Mom was so sad about it. My mother would stand to the side in sadness and shame wishing she could provide enough to eat for her family. My older siblings threw the smaller ones into the dumpster, warning us not to slip on the lettuce and joking about what we might find. In the dumpster, I would toss out food as my older siblings caught it and put it in an old grocery cart we took from the store. We always returned the cart after we walked our food treasures home.

I grew up knowing what day the stores threw out treats from their bakery. I would go search for sugary snacks, even though the cookies and cakes would be stale. Living as food-insecure as we did caused my mother to be quite creative; if she couldn't make the stale, almost-rotten food taste good, we would go hungry. My mother used to toast very stale hot dog buns in the oven, slather peanut butter on them, and call them *rusks*. She said it was a French treat, and we were lucky to have them. We would celebrate with tea parties of rusks and water.

Eventually, we left that house in Champaign—we couldn't afford it. The nine of us moved to a house the size of a shed, but we were only there for a short while. One day, the sump pump broke, the house flooded, and most of our belongings were ruined. It was then that my mom left my abusive dad. She wasn't afraid of leaving because it meant she had one less mouth to feed.

The eight of us went to an apartment in Champaign. Our building was burned down by a nineteen-year-old kid who was playing with a fire that got out of hand.

Several times, I was homeless, but even when I had a

place to stay, it was never *home*. I felt unwanted, covered in the filth of my mother's hoarding, her shame, and our secrets, and oftentimes my physical security was threatened.

I was told over and over I would never amount to anything, but I've always had a deep knowledge that I was created for more, a belief that I'm worth it. I know I have forgotten that from time to time over the years, but I never let despair take over for long—I always try to look at the world with a positive view.

"THE CHALLENGE IS NOT TO BE PERFECT . . .
IT'S TO BE WHOLE."
—JANE FONDA

Today I like to think of myself as a bruised up rotten banana that was changed into sweet banana bread. I was the ragamuffin, the throw-away kid. A projects child on the welfare line. No one—not even me—had any expectation for my life to amount to anything.

But it did.

And now I am happy to continually surprise those people as well as myself!

Now, my life is not about having enough money or

food, like it was when I was a child. It's about living in a place of joy, peace, and happiness. Today I live in over-flowing abundance and am able to joyfully provide for my family and those in need around me.

My life has been transformed. Now I am a business owner, an international speaker, and a life coach that gets to influence thousands of people a year in a positive way. In this book, I want to share with you how you can take the truth of your past and prove to yourself and others that you can be the exception, not the rule.

In this book, you won't find any magic solutions; instead, you'll be introduced to a series of choices that teach you to look forward, be kind to yourself, and be inspired by others so that you can learn from them in meaningful ways.

Let my book take you on a journey to find and embrace your exceptional life!

STEP 1

Be Honest

"No matter how difficult and painful it may be, nothing sounds as good to the soul as the truth."
—Martha Beck

My mother's hoarding was always bad, but in a house of seven children, it became even worse. My house was literally a garbage dump; it reeked, and because we lived there, we reeked. I was musty, patched together. I felt like I was nearing my own expiration date.

Our house was filled with stuff. Some of it had value,

but most of it was junk. The floor to the ceiling was piled high with old papers, boxes, and an overall excess of everything. There was no room for anything else—no place to sit or be safe.

For those who don't suffer from the compulsion to hoard, it's hard to understand. Even I have trouble, and I grew up with it. I wish I could put it in simple terms, but the truth is, there is nothing simple about it. It is a strange and rarely diagnosed disease.

Simple, normal activities were completely overwhelming for my hoarding mother. Throwing a piece of paper away could cause an emotional breakdown—like she was throwing away a part of herself. I would sometimes try to clean, but I never got far before her panic forced me to stop. I couldn't even *ask* to clean or organize or straighten a stack of papers without getting grounded, even in my own space.

On top of hoarding, my mother suffered from depression and anxiety. *Stuff* was the one thing she had control over; when her house was disrupted, she cried easily and became overwhelmed. She couldn't control her husband, their money, or her seven kids, but collecting things seemed to help.

I am grateful we never had pets because it would have made living conditions even worse. I used to lie in bed at night listening to the mice crawl around me, and I would cry myself to sleep wishing that there could be more to my life. In the midst of a household full of filth, I was shameful of and angry at not having enough of what I needed and too much of what I didn't. There were too many of us kids for us to get adequate attention; I was consumed by fear and loneliness. I felt like less than nothing. Less than the blank pieces of paper my mom loved and hung on to. My heart broke and longed for what other kids had. I prayed that someday I could experience a *normal* family, whatever that looked and felt like.

Our days were about surviving, not living.

All I thought about was getting by, just getting through one more day. I was always holding my breath, hoping no one would see the pain and sorrow that lived behind my fake smile. Every aspect of our home was chaotic—there was no schedule, no security, and no one happy to see us when we came home. All my siblings and I had to fight for food, personal space, a moment of quiet. We were kept isolated. Because of my mother's shame and compulsion to hoard, she insisted that no one ever come in. If someone came to pick us up, we had to quickly run out to the car. In my mother's mind, keeping our lives and the way we lived secret was the most important.

It was the secretiveness that made my living situation bad. It kept me from recognizing that other people were going through some of the same things we were going through. It kept us from realizing that my mother's hoarding and anxiety and depression were mental illnesses.

A few years ago, I came across the TV show *Hoarders*. It was a weekend marathon, and I sat in front of the TV frozen, crying. My husband, Greg, kept asking me what I was doing; I had never really watched TV, but I was becoming obsessed with this show. I couldn't help myself; viewing the show overwhelmed me with a flood of different emotions.

At first, I felt relief and a sense of joy that other people lived like I did. I wasn't alone anymore. It was an actual disease, like addiction, and it required help. After an hour or so, I went from relief to overwhelming sadness that other people in this world live with this horrible secret in a lonely, depressed environment filled with garbage and piles and piles of stuff.

There's a freedom in learning that you or someone you love is suffering from some sort of mental illness. When there's an explanation, there's less shame. Hoarding is a mental illness. That is the truth. Yet my mother has never acknowledged that she has a problem or an illness, and she has never admitted that a literal dump was a bad place to raise a family.

"Owning our story can be hard
but not nearly as difficult as spending
our lives running from it."
—Brené Brown

It took me a long time to break out of the cycle of secrets, to believe that I deserved an exceptional life free from anxiety and secrets designed to hide my mother's illness from everyone, including herself.

I couldn't move forward past a childhood of secrets and mental illness until I could own this history and see it as truth instead of just explaining it away. As a child, I was convinced everything was okay and was stuck living in a day-to-day cycle of surviving. But labels don't need to be a self-fulfilling prophecy. I didn't need to let the hoarding, depression, loneliness, abandonment, and feelings of being under-valued consume me; but I also couldn't pretend it didn't happen. I had to figure out that it wasn't okay how I was forced to live as a child—in a household where stuff meant more than kids, family, and stability—and then move on.

My mother went to a support group for hoarders once

in the last few years—at age eighty-five—because her social worker told her to. Afterwards, she told me that everyone there had serious problems and were severely messed up. But never once did she say that she needed to be there, or that she, too, was going through what they were going through. She baked a cake for the group because they needed help and she was there to be kind and benevolent, rather than to get help herself. Her truth was that she was fine; it was the world that was broken. She was normal, and everyone else had problems and was wasteful. These lies became my truth as a child.

> "SPEAK AND SEEK TRUTH TO FIND YOUR
> OWN TRUTH."
> —ANNIE MEEHAN

When people struggle, whether from mental illness, depression, or just terrible life circumstances, it's easy for them to shift their realities to make them fit their worlds and help them make it through the day-to-day. These false realities can have strong impacts even on those who aren't struggling themselves. If you're constantly hearing lies from someone you love, you might break, over and over, until you feel so low you can't remember what the truth looks and feels like. In my case, this false reality, my mother's reality, was that I was worth less than the garbage that polluted our home. My exposure to my mother's reality made it my reality as well, and I had no one to tell me these things were lies.

I knew a woman once who, more than anything, wanted to be married, to be loved. She thought it would give her value or significance. She kept attracting the wrong kind of men—after all, they say that if you are too desperate looking for love, you will find it in all the wrong places with all the wrong people. But she was willing to settle for less than a satisfactory relationship because she didn't want to be alone.

Her first husband ignored her most of the time. When he did pay her any attention, he told her she was boring and unattractive. After a few years, he left her for someone else.

She met another man who was kinder, more exciting, and more fun. But a few months into their relationship, he became controlling. He was hot-tempered and blamed his childhood and his first wife for his anger. He was an alcoholic, and he kept this woman from seeing her friends. He would call her names, tell her that she was lucky to have him and that no one else would want her.

....

"YOU BECOME WHAT YOU BELIEVE."
—OPRAH WINFREY

....

Reading this, I'm sure you're asking why she didn't just leave—after all, these are big red flags. But she had low self-esteem and wanted so much to be loved, and when you want that, it's easy to excuse the bad behavior of your spouse and start to blame yourself for the abuse, start to think that you did something to make him act this way.

He insisted she needed plastic surgery to make her body more attractive. She didn't want it but went along with it anyway. They got married, but didn't invite any of her friends to the wedding. In reality, it was more of a funeral than a celebration. She lived like this for a number of years, though friends and professionals encouraged her to leave and told her she deserved more. But she didn't believe them. She would move out for a bit and then return, and her husband would be sweet and kind at first, and then angry, mean, and controlling. As time went on, he became more and more aggressive. She would hide from him, but when he found her, he would throw her out of the house. Sometimes, she would go quietly; other times, she would stand her ground. Either way, she always went back to him. He was depressed and an alcoholic, and she took those ailments to be her own, trying to fix him—and by doing so, fix herself.

Once, when he told her to get out, she went to the basement instead. He began to yell, and so she hid in the closet. It was just a normal night. He found her, dragged her out of the closet, and broke her arm. Even though she was in pain, she still felt bad for him, and her heart broke because of his suffering. She felt compassion for this despondent, stressed, and broken man who hadn't gotten help for his depression.

She held herself together until her arm swelled so large she had no choice but to go to the ER. The radiologists asked what happened and begged her to report him, if not to save herself, then for the next woman.

She ended up calling a friend and asking her to please help file a police report. They drove together and the tears flowed as she shared her story and the detective wrote down all the details. A number of times she explained to the officer what she might have done wrong and how it was probably her fault. But he told her it was not her fault. It had never been her fault.

But a few days later, she got scared and canceled the charges. This woman had been told so many times that she was unworthy of love that it became true in her eyes. She still isn't convinced she was wrong. I hope she will realize it someday, because recognizing the truth is a miracle.

Knowing the truth can make you feel good about yourself, give you the confidence to take a step toward a life you really want, or it could potentially save your life, like the woman in the story above. Knowing the truth has saved lives.

My friend Wendy told me a story from her time as a substitute host on a local radio station. On the air one evening, she asked: "Have you ever witnessed a miracle in your life?" A man named John called in.

In a calm, confident, baritone voice, John told the audience that by the time he was twenty-eight years old, he had won and lost everything. He was an uncontrolled alcoholic, having been through treatment several times to no avail. His wife had left him and taken their kids, he got fired, and he lost his house.

John confessed that he was going to end his life. He made a plan to drive to a town he didn't know, pull off onto a side road where he'd never been, and shoot himself with a borrowed pistol. The day he decided to die, he pulled into the back of a gravel parking lot behind a building he didn't know.

There, John played with the pistol in his hand when he remembered something one of his chemical dependency counselors—a man he had hated—had said: "If you think that ending your addiction by suicide is the only route you can take, that's fine. However, have enough respect for yourself to take that action ONLY if you spend one minute—and I mean sixty full, focused seconds—to think about your actions and the outcome. If after that one focused minute you still believe this is the only way, then you're not making a snap decision, so go ahead and do it."

John hated that counselor. Hated his voice, his words, and his attitude . . . so it was even more hateful that these were the last thoughts he would ever think. So he decided to do his sixty seconds before shooting himself. Easy, right? Wrong.

Across the parking lot, there was a door that was slightly ajar, and thin light was coming through it. Curiosity destroyed his concentration, and he had to start his one minute all over again. But it was no good. John's eyes kept darting to the light that was growing stronger as the night got darker and darker.

Cursing himself as a failure even in suicide, John decided to get out and investigate what was distracting him, so that once he knew the source of the annoying light, he could do his full sixty seconds.

As John approached the door, he said, he was about to reach for the handle when it suddenly swung open and a hopeful man appeared. The man gently asked, "Are you here for the Alcoholics Anonymous meeting?"

He was.

At that exact moment, the walls came down. This road he didn't know, in this city that he'd never visited, with a gun that wasn't his, delivered him to the stoop of the very thing he was running from. John shared with his new friend that he was out of control, had lost everything, and had a loaded pistol in the car.

That night, John started to get his life back. His job, his house, his self-respect, wife, and kids—all because a CD counselor whose guts he hated had spoken the truth into him before he was ready to hear it.

Then John finished the call by saying, "If you don't think that's a miracle, I don't know what is." And he quietly wished her well and hung up the phone.

John's truth was that he was an addict, and that his disease was ruining his life. The truth was that John was able to look beyond suicide—an easy out—and work hard to get back the things in his life that mattered. The truth was that he wasn't helpless. He just needed help.

Once, after I had given a talk about truth, a woman came up to me and said, "Thank you. You offered me freedom today. I have a mentally ill family member that always says I was mean to him growing up. I wasn't, and so when he says that I always argue, because I don't want him to think I'm a terrible person. But today, I realized that I don't have to convince him. I just have to know that I was kind."

When you know the truth—and I mean the real truth, not the lies you believe to be true—you don't have to convince anyone else or get agreement. For years, I pleaded with my mom to get her to acknowledge how we lived and the painful things she said to me. I wanted someone else to verify that it was true. But she always told me I made it all up. I found total freedom when I realized I didn't need her to agree with me. She could have her story, and I could have my truth, which is that she might have done her best, but she was sick, and to her, I was not good enough. I can live with that truth and still know that I was, and am, good enough.

"IS THERE A DIFFERENCE BETWEEN YOUR
TRUTH AND THE TRUTH?"
—ANNIE MEEHAN

The woman whose husband broke her arm thought her truth was that she did things to make her husband angry and she was punished for them, often excessively, and it was okay if he hurt her, because he didn't mean to and because she deserved the punishment. But that's a lie. The real truth is that no one has the right to hurt you. It doesn't matter why they do it or what their excuses are. The truth is that it's wrong. Excuses, if we tell them to ourselves enough, become our truth. They are the lies we tell ourselves.

If you don't start with the truth, it's easy to be confused, manipulated, and controlled. If you spend your life internalizing a lie, you're going to convince yourself that you're never good enough, smart enough, or worth enough.

When people think negatively about us, what they're really doing is attaching a label to us—unlovable, mean, or stupid. But it's important to remember that labels are always evolving, and they're not true. As a kid, my brothers and sisters and I did a lot of bad things, but we weren't bad kids like we were labeled. We just made a bad choice in a single moment because we didn't have anyone parenting us.

When I was nineteen, I went to an office in downtown Minneapolis to interview for a scholarship for college. A few minutes into the interview, the interviewer stopped me and asked once more for my name. Then he held up my application and asked if it was mine. It was.

He looked confused and said, "I can't believe you're the person who wrote this. This application is not good. It's filled with half-formed thoughts and misspelled words. I thought it was written by someone who was illiterate.

But here you are, articulate and bright. How did this happen?"

I explained that I was dyslexic, and that reading and writing were very, very hard for me. But that did not mean I was stupid. It just meant that I was smart in other ways. He had labeled me illiterate, and I could have let that define me—as stupid, as unfit for college—or I could realize that he simply didn't have the whole story and that my own label for myself was far more fierce and far more accurate. I let my own label—as a fighter, a survivor, the one who beat all the odds—become my truth. And here I am, dyslexic and publishing a book.

"YOU ARE THE ONE THAT POSSESSES THE KEYS
TO YOUR BEING. YOU CARRY THE PASSPORT
TO YOUR OWN HAPPINESS."
—DIANE VON FURSTENBERG

The biggest truth I had to learn—and one that I'm still learning every single day—is that my mother did her best to love her children, but the truth is that we rarely felt loved, supported, or valued. Because we did not get encouragement at home, it was hard to feel like we were worth the respect and love out in the world. Many of us ended up in unhealthy and abusive relationships.

But this is the truth:

The truth is that my childhood was filled with struggles, tragedy, and sadness.

It was not my fault.

I deserved better.

You deserve better!

It is not your fault when you are abused, neglected, or unloved.

I am not bitter anymore. But I will acknowledge the truth so I can break the cycle of an unhealthy life and live free from unhealthy lies we think are true and sometimes become the truth. No one deserves abuse or neglect. We all deserve to be loved, seen, and treated with respect.

You don't have to repeat your cycle, or be hard on yourself because you're in a tough situation.

You can be the Exception and live a different, happy life.

Reframe your thinking, little by little, step by step.

Not everything has to be perfect. Things are messy and always will be. But even in the mess and pain, you can say to yourself, **"I will not stay here suffocated by lies, dysfunction, and hurt. I will break free!"**

You might be scared. I was, and I still am some days. Chaos can be a kind of sanctuary, all that keeps you going; but while a chaotic life may mask your pain, it won't ever give you true peace and happiness. I spent the first half of my life holding my breath, waiting to make it through one moment and into the next. I was in crisis mode, and it kept me from realizing the truth of my situation. Instead, I was always paying attention to the lies running through my head.

"QUIET CAN BE SCARY, BUT THAT'S WHEN
THE TRUTH SEEPS IN."
—ANNIE MEEHAN

The quiet times are when you can slow down and figure out what to do and how to move forward. You will have greater success in all areas of your life if you change your attitude, clean up your mental messages, and choose to change.

Here are a few examples of the lies we tell ourselves, what truth we should really be focusing on, and how to move forward.

The lie: Alcohol makes me happy, that's why I drink. I don't have a problem.

The truth: I am addicted to alcohol, and I am not happy.

Moving forward: I am going to seek support in regaining independence from alcohol.

———◆●◆———

The lie: I had a bad childhood because I was a bad child.

The truth: I was a troubled (not bad) child because my childhood lacked support and encouragement, and I wasn't raised with parents the way other children were.

Moving forward: I acknowledge that my circumstances weren't the best. Everyone did the best they could when I was growing up, but I needed more support at that time in my life. I will do my best to learn from this and give my children a better, more exceptional life than I had.

The lie: Suffering is a part of everyday life.

The truth: There will be some suffering in my life, but there will also be some joy.

Moving forward: I will focus on the good so when the pain comes it will not overtake me.

The lie: You have no value, no gifts, no strengths. You are worthless.

The truth: You have weaknesses, but you also have abundant gifts and strengths.

Moving forward: I will work on building my strengths and seek help with any weakness. I am valuable and have gifts worth sharing.

Your turn:

———●•●———

Your lie: _____

_____

Your truth: _____

_____

Moving forward: _____

_____

———●•●———

Your lie: _____

_____

Your truth: _____

_____

Moving forward: _____

_____

— •• —

Your lie: _____

_____

Your truth: _____

_____

Moving forward: _____

_____

— •• —

Your lie: _____

_____

Your truth: _____

_____

Moving forward: _____

_____

———•●●•———

Your lie: _____

_____

Your truth: _____

_____

Moving forward: _____

_____

STEP 2

Be Open

"I HAVE STOOD ON A MOUNTAIN OF
NOS FOR ONE YES."
—B. SMITH

When I was seven years old, my mom took us kids and left our dad and our flooded white house. After that, he became a drop-in dad who would appear only now and again. My mom gave us life, but that was about all she was able to provide; she couldn't love or nurture us in the ways we needed. I often dreamt about what it would have felt like to have parents who taught me how to love, nurture, cook, wear makeup, clean, entertain, pray, read the Bible, be honest, study hard, and believe in myself. My mom did the best job she could, but so many things overwhelmed her to the point of debilitating her. She was independent ("I'll do this if it kills me!") and physically strong, but emotionally wounded. She never asked for help when she needed it, and we suffered for it.

About five years ago, my dad died. I had not seen him for over twenty-five years. He had been a transient, living on the street and moving from place to place. He had spent the last few years homeless in Juarez, Mexico, drinking himself to death.

A few weeks before he passed away, a couple from one of the local Catholic churches of Juarez felt called by God to help my dad, so they invited him to live with them. When he died, they worked hard to find us and wrote a letter to my family in Spanish. They said that he was a very grumpy man, always angry except when he was around their two kids, even though he normally hated all kids.

We wanted to ship his cremated body back to the US, and my mom, sisters, and I all chipped in for it. During this time, something interesting happened: I had a deep desire to have a funeral. He created me but never raised me, and I needed closure with a man who had only ever inflicted pain in my life.

I suffered from great grief after his passing. I was buried in sorrow not because of his absence, but because he had always been absent. I grieved for what wasn't and what would never be. I am a hopeless romantic and had always hoped that someday he would reappear in my life to love and care about me.

I allowed myself to get lost in the sadness; I lived in my pink robe for days after the funeral. The hardest part in the process was that no one understood how I could be so sad for the loss of a dad I had never had. The people who I thought would be there (my bible study friends) did not check in; no one sent a card; two friends showed up to sit with me for a little while, but I still felt alone and unloved.

After a few weeks of sitting alone in the kitchen or on the couch in my pink robe, my daughter came home with two friends. It was after midnight, but they sat with me and asked me questions about him and how I was feeling and tried to understand my loss, my pain, and my confused feelings about never having the dad I had longed for.

After a while, they stopped me and said, "That's it. Let's go to Perkins and get some pancakes." It was two in the morning at this point, and I said no thanks. I didn't even have the energy to get dressed. So they went upstairs.

In two minutes, they were all back down, dressed in robes. They told me that if I couldn't change out of the robe, then they were going to change into robes! So we all went to Perkins at two a.m. and got pancakes and laughed and cried together.

Sometimes, when life hits you hard, you don't need someone to pull you out of the pit. You just need them to jump down into it and join you in a robe.

That early-morning pancake run was such a blessing. Our kids can be our teachers, our support, and our guides. My daughter and her friends were eighteen and wise beyond their years, and they blessed me with their love and support. The next day, I was able to get up and start taking better care of myself. I was able to let go of the past (and the past I never had) and move forward and focus on the family I had created.

> "MANY HANDS AND HEARTS LESSEN THE LOAD
> YOU CARRY ON THE PATH TO HEALING."
> —ANNIE MEEHAN

Like many people, I was born with a mother and a father who created my biological family. But beyond that, the working definition of my family has been more of a creative writing project with unbelievable twists and turns. When I was growing up, my family was never enough for many reasons. Our mother never asked for help in taking care of us, so as children, we didn't have a familial structure—which meant we barely had a family. We lived in a riot of confusion, unsure where we would get our next meals, whether or not we would have a place to sleep, if anyone would ever see us for the people we were beyond our circumstances.

At a very young age, I started creating "families" for myself in order to fill the void. A family would emerge when I went to a girlfriend's house for the whole weekend because it was where I had meals, parents, structure, and stability.

These "families" were ever changing, but they were my first support systems. I grew up in crisis mode, only living from one second to the next. When I found these families, I could transition into survival mode because I could finally rely on someone. Being able to trust gives you a reason to move forward towards thriving.

As I've grown, I've realized that I must define my own family. I do not live in a world where family has come to me naturally, and I know that nurturing love cannot be taken for granted. For many, this kind of love is as natural as breathing. But if you have never had nurturing love, it is a different story. It has been difficult, but I have come to understand that I do not have to be defined by the minimal love that my mother could sparingly afford. I do not have to follow blood rites in the naming of my own family. I can choose the love I believe I deserve. These realizations have been liberating.

No matter how healthy and functional you are as a person, you are not meant to go through life alone. This doesn't mean that you need a spouse and children, but you do need people who can support you, give advice, love, and anything else you might need to be a strong, happy person.

Usually, humans only reach out to get help when there's an emergency, but that's not the only time you need support. It's important to keep filling your life with problem solvers, friends, and fans, even when you think you don't need them or deserve them.

Some people, especially if they were raised in an environment that wasn't supportive, might believe that needing and asking for help is weak.

It's not.

It takes strength to know where and when we need support and courage to accept help when someone else recognizes that you need support.

Accepting support is not a failure. It is a privilege. It is a privilege to share this life with people who love you enough to be there when you need them. Not everyone has that.

I grew up without a stable family, feeling like less than nothing, deprived of love and confidence. I never thought I would be sitting where I am sitting today. But I have worked with others to grow past those hindrances, and because of the support I have, I feel like I am blooming daily, emerging into the world from my cocoon as beautiful as I was created to be.

"AND THE DAY CAME WHEN THE RISK TO REMAIN TIGHT IN A BUD WAS MORE PAINFUL THAN THE RISK IT TOOK TO BLOSSOM."
—ANAÏS NIN

The first step to thriving and living in joy is to surround yourself with positive people—your first version of your family.

I am sure you have heard this advice before, but I'm saying it again: you need to surround yourself with people who believe in *you* and *your potential.*

There are important reasons for this. These people:

- Believe we are created for *more*, even when we *forget.*
- Know that our purpose is even bigger than ourselves.
- Build us up when we have an off day and never shame us.
- Encourage us and remind us we don't have to be perfect to believe in ourselves.
- Are soul friends; they fill us up, not drain us.
- Give us more balance, keeping our lows and highs from getting too extreme.
- Remind us not to take ourselves too seriously. We laugh with and at each other because life is more fun with friends.

> "MAKE THE MOST OF YOURSELF BY FANNING THE TINY, INNER SPARKS OF POSSIBILITY INTO FLAMES OF ACHIEVEMENT."
> —GOLDA MEIR

Asking for help really is the key to success, whether you do it fairly regularly or only occasionally. It keeps you from hurting yourself and others by trying to handle everything alone. It also keeps you humble and aware that you are not perfect. You need others, as we all do! It allows you to embrace imperfection and pick yourself up more easily after a failure.

Remember that a perfectionist always goes to sleep a little disappointed or frustrated that everything did not turn out the way they wanted or imagined. But someone like me accepts that life can be a little messy, and that's part of the process. I go to bed grateful that I only messed up five times today instead of ten, and I sleep soundly knowing I am willing to make amends for those mistakes tomorrow.

Some people might think that if you've reached out for help from one person, that's enough; but I like to look for help from every source. If you don't think you have enough of a support system with friends or family (or you don't feel comfortable asking for more support), explore other options.

Sometimes, it's much scarier to admit you need help to the people close to you than it is to a stranger. If you're not ready, or you don't think you'd get an encouraging response, feel free to look further out. The American Counseling Association, Al-Anon and NAMI are wonderful support groups, and most churches have support networks that cover multiple situations.

When I was fifteen, I was forced to look outside my home for support for the first time. My single mother, four of my siblings (one had left for college, and one had gone to live with a friend and never came back), and I were living in South Minneapolis, all together after a year of living apart in the homes of kind near-strangers and relatives. One day when Mom came home from work, she seemed more stressed than usual. The boys were fighting over the TV, and one of my sisters was yelling because she lost something. When Mom came in the back door to the kitchen, she yelled, *"Get out!"* She meant everyone—she could not take it anymore.

I didn't have a friend's house to go to, and all I could think of was walking the six blocks to The Bridge for Runaway Youth. Today, The Bridge is a safe haven for any kid in Minneapolis and Chanhassen, but then, it was a short-term shelter, a place I could go and only stay for a few days. I had no idea if The Bridge could actually offer the support I needed; I was sad and scared, but I had no other choice.

The walk there was the loneliest walk of my life, but

once I got to The Bridge, I immediately felt *safe*. Bill, the director, made me feel special by listening to me and to my story. He made me feel like a person, an exception, instead of just another troubled kid. He told me I would be okay, and things would work out. Unlike my house, The Bridge was clean and comfortable. It had rules, structure, and plenty of food—all things unfamiliar to me.

The Bridge became my home away from home over the next few years whenever my mother got overwhelmed and wanted us out of the house. I ended up there four different times. For months after my stays, I attended a weekly aftercare group that focused on surviving post-crisis. It was a safe and encouraging place for me to go each week to share, listen, and learn. There, I could think about the good in my life, not just the struggles. I met two of my best friends in that support group, and we are still friends to this day.

Bill set me up with Nancy, a personal mentor. We met weekly for lunch after I had gone home, and she shared her own struggles and her strengths. She would encourage me, even though I continued to struggle, displaying all kinds of destructive behavior. I didn't feel worth it, and I didn't believe I deserved good in my life. I had low self-esteem, I was drinking, and I was depressed. But she was there, even though I would take two steps forward and one step back.

Because of the support and the resources The Bridge set me up with, I found three part-time jobs, a place to live, and finished my education. At age seventeen, I received my General Education Diploma (I had dropped out of school two months before graduating). As time went by, I continued to go back to The Bridge, this time to mentor other kids and teens in the support group.

Since my time there, The Bridge has grown. It is still located in the same house, but now it occupies a large building across the street as well. It also provides housing for teens to stay at for up to a year. Volunteers go out looking for teens on the street and offer them shelter. I've spoken on behalf of The Bridge to both give back and raise awareness—most people don't realize that runaways don't always run away!

The Bridge is only one example of an establishment that changed my life; there are so many options of places outside of friends and family where you can find support (either physical or emotional) to help you along your journey. Think about professional resources: counseling, coaching, support groups, prayer groups, and support hotlines, just to name a few.

Counseling

Many people think going to counseling or therapy is a sign of weakness or failure—that you're crazy, nuts, or naughty. In reality, it is a sign of strength. By accepting that you don't have all the answers and don't have it all together and opening yourself up to other ideas and a new perspective, you're growing and putting yourself in a better position to deal with your issues, whatever they may be. We are told that we have to do it all—especially us women—and it's important to remember that we're not bad people, friends, mothers, daughters, sisters, or workers for not being able to always cover everything. Sometimes things fall outside of our control. It's healthy to be able to admit when you need help.

Therapy options are plentiful: you can do one-on-one sessions with a counselor, psychologist, or psychiatrist. You can go to group therapy, where you partner with others like yourself along your journey. You can also attend support groups to help you keep your progress in check and encourage you to make good choices and create healthy habits.

If you feel that going to therapy—either individual or group—could be even the slightest bit helpful, give it a fair shake. You might not love everyone and you might not gel with their stories and situations, but remember that they might have something to teach you, or they may need you in their life to shine a light onto their situation. At the very least, you'll see that you are truly not alone in your situation.

I love to encourage people to try counseling for six weeks. That's six times before you can decide if it's a good fit or not. Most likely, it will be!

Faith

If you don't yet belong to a faith community where you feel comfortable, consider joining a congregation at a church, synagogue, or mosque. Make sure that you're looking for a place that feels supportive, welcoming, and nonjudgmental. It will be easier for you to open up and seek help if you feel comfortable from the beginning. Research the programming of your church or temple and make sure that you won't just get lost in the crowd. If you are Christian, look into Celebrate Recovery, which is a great program hosted by many churches!

If you already belong to a congregation you like, you can ask the pastor, priest, rabbi, or leader to meet with you one-on-one. Many religious establishments have support groups, mentor programs, and more.

Coaching and Training

This can include many different services—personal trainers, life coaches, or other people who can advise you.

If you have depression, are feeling ill, or have low self-confidence, personal trainers can help you get your physical body healthy again. Exercise helps reduce the effects of depression by flooding your body with endorphins. Seeing changes in your body might boost your self-confidence, and being healthier overall will make it easier to think positively and reframe your worldview!

Personal trainers also teach goal setting, and setting goals with your health can quickly snowball into setting goals for other aspects of your life!

A life coach takes what a personal trainer does to your body and focuses it on other parts of your life as well. If you want to work on multiple areas of your life at once, a life coach can be the perfect holistic solution.

As a life coach, I work with clients in transition, whether it be a career change, a change in a relationship, or a health transition. Life coaches are trained to help you take the steps to make that change and make sure that that new stage in life is going from good to great!

Other Resources

Many people like to individually work on themselves. Books (like this one) can be a great jumping-off place to add support strategies to your own toolbox. Consider looking at books on how to think positively, how to maintain a healthy lifestyle, or how to understand others.

You can also go to people in your life—friends, family, colleagues, mentors—and ask them to form an advisory board. An advisory board is a team of people who actively foster mutually beneficial relationships. Set up a time every month to meet and trade stories of your strengths, weaknesses, and progress. This will teach you to learn from everyone, whether they are where you are today, where you want to be in five years, or where you were yesterday.

I bought my first house when I was a single parent, and there was another single mother whose house was across the street. We were both working hard to make ends meet and lived paycheck to paycheck. To help share the stress of our lives, we met a few times a week to cook dinner together and talk and exchange stories, life tips, and new discoveries. We would also take turns cooking for each other's children during the week to give the other woman time to catch up on herself. Think about trying to make connections with people who are in a similar place in life as yourself and fostering supportive relationships.

When you are feeling stronger and more valuable after surrounding yourself with positive resources that build you up instead of tear you down, it might be time to take a bigger risk.

Invite someone new to hang out. Start making better, healthier friendships. Maybe add dating back into your life if you've been waiting. Be patient with yourself; it takes time and trust to build strong, lasting relationships. Don't worry about being perfect for others or think you can't learn from people who haven't quite made it. Everyone has broken pieces, and it's not a bad thing.

> "IT'S ONLY WHEN WE FIT OUR PIECES TOGETHER AND LIFT EACH OTHER UP THAT WE CAN HEAL THE CRACKS."
> —ANNIE MEEHAN

As you surround yourself with people who help build you up, you'll find that to get to a truly joyful place, you have to recruit one last person to your side: yourself! Others can't do it all for us—we must start to believe in ourselves.

You can take in as much positive reinforcement from the people around you as you can, but at the end of the day, if you can't stop that negative voice in your head, you won't get too far.

Forgive yourself and others for flaws and mistakes. I often meet people who speak so harshly about themselves that it just breaks my heart. I want to say, "Take away all your *should-have could-have* talk, start speaking truth, and believe in yourself." You are good. Let's write down three things you do right, or three things that are going right, and go from there. You have done more good than bad; you have had failures, but let's focus for a minute on your successes.

Your mind might say you've never:
- Written a book
- Been paid X amount per year
- Finished college
- Found a life partner

Or tell you:
- Life rarely works out for others, why do you think it will work for you?
- You can't do this
- You are not worth anything

But this is fear talking. It's your insecurity.
How will you respond?

For every one negative, it takes five positives to bounce back. To bring back the positive, say:

- I can write 100 words today. If I keep this up, I will have a book.
- I am worth every penny I make and more. I work hard and give it my all.
- I am a life-long learner. I read, watch TED Talks, and take classes.
- I will take care of me, and that will attract a healthy relationship.

Tell yourself:

- Life will work out for me. I am the exception!
- I can do anything I put my mind to!
- I am worth all the love and joy in the world!

How about, **"I will make it this time because I am committed, I am capable, I am able, I am willing, and I want to succeed."**

Now repeat this exercise four times with details specific to yourself. Write them down, and when you're feeling like you can't accomplish your goals, reread them. Try to make a habit of writing down five positives for every negative you think about yourself—soon you'll have a journal of just how wonderful you are!

"GARBAGE IN, GARBAGE OUT.
BE CAREFUL WHAT YOU LISTEN TO, READ,
SPEAK ABOUT YOURSELF, AND SEE."
—ANNIE MEEHAN

Once you have been receiving support long enough to have changed your own mindset, you will eventually get to a point where you will begin to overflow and start wanting to give support as well as receive it.

Go out of your way to be kind, be thoughtful, or thank people for the simple things they do. I often ask clients, "When was the last time you thanked your boss for your job?" If my client is the boss, I ask, "When was the last time you appreciated your employees for simple things like showing up on time or finishing a project by a deadline, or more notable things like going way beyond expectations?" Sometimes people just need a few kind words to change an attitude or an environment. When it comes to our spouse or children, it is easy to focus on our to-do list or on what they missed doing, but it is so important to build them up with our words and our actions. Did they get a report card with three As or with one D? Where do you focus? On the struggle in your life or the success?

Give back to the people who have given to you. Give back to the people who don't expect it and who haven't given. I always wanted to be a speaker, to be able to reach and influence people with my words and help them inspire positive changes in their own lives, but it didn't happen overnight. I didn't even make it happen on my own. I needed to get a jump-start from someone who was full enough to give back to others—to me—before I could take that step myself.

I was working as a lunch lady in a public school when I met an insurance salesman. We joined together to create a networking group so I could grow my AdvoCare business. I had been in a larger networking group, but the meetings were always scheduled during meal times, and that's when I was working. So he and I created this networking group that met at two in the afternoon, and over time it grew from two people to over thirty. We had fun, we learned a lot, and we supported each other.

One day, a woman asked me if I was happy as a lunch lady and an AdvoCare adviser. She asked if I was doing what I really wanted. I told her about my hopes and dream of speaking on a stage and influencing millions of people and building them up, to be authentic, to make a difference. I was willing to do whatever it took to get there, but I also doubted myself and hadn't taken many steps to make my dream happen.

But my new friend believed in me and in my talent of connecting with people. The next time I saw her at networking, she told me she had something for me. She had created a flyer for my speaking career; it was a trifold filled with pictures, quotes, and even speaking topics. I was incredibly moved by her gesture. I asked her where she had gotten all of it. She said that she had gotten the information from my Facebook and LinkedIn profiles, and that I was already inspiring people to be better than they think they can be or were in the past. Then she told me that she believed in me.

I was shocked, touched, moved to tears even, that someone would take the time to care about me enough to create this. There was nothing in it for her, she just believed in herself enough to be able to support and believe in me too, enough to reach out and give more. So often in life someone else can see our good and our worth before we see it in ourselves.

If you're feeling overwhelmed about how to seek help, begin asking yourself these things:

Which friend or family member do I feel supports me?

_____

I think I would like to make connections at _____

_____ organization.

Who am I not close with now, but could become a posi-

tive addition to my life? _____

_____

I am good at _____,

so I could help others with _____

I might need help with _____

so _____ can become a reality.

I dream of someday becoming _____

_____

I want to make a difference in the world by _____

_____

I want my legacy to be _____

_____

STEP 3

Be Healthy

"THE QUESTION ISN'T WHO'S GOING TO
LET ME; IT'S WHO IS GOING TO STOP ME."
—AYN RAND

Often I work with clients who are waiting until they
have a little more time or a little more money before they can start taking care of themselves. They think,
*Once the kids get older, when I get a new job with a less
demanding boss, when my husband travels less—then I will
make time for myself.* But you can't wait. We do a disser-
vice to ourselves and everyone around us when we don't

make time to take care of ourselves.

It is your choice to decide when you are ready to start taking care of yourself, but the sooner you start the better you will feel. The first step is deciding that you are sick and tired of being sick and tired. You have to decide you don't want to go through life constantly in search of your real smile. You have to ask yourself the hard questions:

Am I ready to be happy? Can I let go? Can I forgive? Can I honestly look at my past and know that it does not define my future? Is there ever a perfect time? Am I willing to do the work, even on the hard days? Even when I don't feel like it? Can I create a new story, a new mindset?

Start slowly, one step at a time, but start today—don't put it off any longer. You are worth it, and as you take care of yourself, you will offer hope to others around you.

I was at an Al-Anon conference when I heard a woman tell a wonderful story about self-care. She had just gotten a messy and painful divorce from an alcoholic and was beginning to be encouraged to date again. She was reluctant, but with a little push from a good friend, she agreed to go on a blind date.

She had a good time, but at the end of the night, her date told her that she could never be higher than third on his list of priorities. Now, this woman had a marketing and sales background, and she responded that he wasn't marketing himself very well and his sales pitch wasn't doing much for getting him a second date. But then he explained: first on his list of priorities was his higher power, because his spirituality kept him humble and reminded him that he couldn't handle life all by himself. His next priority was his sobriety, because if he didn't stay clean and take care of himself, he would be no good to anyone else. He didn't mean that he wouldn't care for and love a potential life partner; he just knew that if you take care of yourself first, you make a better partner, as well as a better parent, employee, family member, and friend.

In 2007, I bought my first Snap Fitness workout facility. In the years since, I've met hundreds of people with a long list of excuses as to why they don't have the time, money, or energy to work out. One such person I met was a member of my facility. He really didn't want to come to the gym; in fact, he was a member of the gym for six months before I ever met him (and I almost always meet, or at least recognize, my members). But when I did meet him, he stopped me to tell me his story.

He had weighed 450 pounds and had given up on the idea of ever losing weight. He had even given up on the idea of ever doing anything with his life. He was retired and was happy to sit in his chair at home and just eat chips and drink soda. But then his wife dragged him to Snap Fitness and he met one of our trainers. The gym was the last place he wanted to be, but the trainer encouraged him and believed in him and told him that he could get healthy, get energized, and lose some weight.

When I met him, he had already lost 125 pounds.

The trainer had pushed him through each day and believed in him until he could believe in himself, and now that member is excited to come to the gym. His life is back on track, and he's happy with how he's progressing in his journey. He has his life, his hope, and his belief in himself back. He decided he was worth it.

"IF YOU DON'T LIKE THE ROAD YOU'RE WALKING, START PAVING ANOTHER ONE."
—DOLLY PARTON

Most of you aren't 450 pounds, but even if you're fit, taking care of yourself has many components. It is about giving yourself some sort of schedule you can stick to at least 80 percent. It is about scheduling some downtime to rest, relax, read, and reflect. Making sure you have time for movement to get that heart rate up every day for at least twenty minutes. Having time to menu plan and prepare meals, even if you only do so one day a week. It means making time for family and friends. No one lives in perfect balance, but putting yourself first, getting enough sleep, and having just five minutes of quiet time each day will make you a better spouse, parent, and employer/employee.

As a parent, I know how easy it is to put yourself last and just wear yourself down till you are completely worn out. I see this often in my clients, as well. I know not everyone is a morning person like I am, but even setting that alarm fifteen minutes earlier to take three deep breaths, stretch, and mentally prepare for the day before someone needs your help can keep you going physically and emotionally throughout the day.

One thing I have learned about myself over the years is that if I don't take care of myself by getting enough sleep, moving my body daily, eating healthy, taking my supplements, having adult connections and conversations, and drinking enough water, I will get worn down—and it shows up in all sorts of ugly ways. I might get physically sick, I might be crabby, or I might even get depressed. What I know for sure is little things become big things when I don't feel my best.

Taking care of yourself is not optional if you want to be at A+ best!

When we are vulnerable physically we are much more

self-critical and sensitive. Growing up, I was taught that taking care of myself was selfish and a waste of time—even wanting time alone in the bathroom to shower and do my hair was criticized. But I've learned since then that whatever makes you feel *human* is something you should prioritize and spend time on.

Now, I make sure I shower with a nice body wash—it's a simple treat. As a kid, it was ingrained in me to shower quickly and only use soap on my face. Part of the reason I was taught this was out of need—in a house of eight people, water can get very expensive very quickly. But part of it was that in my family, we didn't think of ourselves as needing or deserving of that care.

My mom thinks women should have short hair and not color it. She taught me that it was a waste of time to do hair or makeup—only selfish women do that, because they want to show off. Sometimes, I still find myself thinking these thoughts, but I deserve to take care of myself and present myself in any way I want, and I've had to retrain myself to think differently about what it means to take care of myself.

When we take care of ourselves first, we are *self-full*. Not selfish. When we take care of ourselves first, we have more to offer those we love.

I coach a client with three little kids. She's a nurse, and she spends her life putting others first. She works full time and takes care of the house and the kids. She came to me feeling extremely guilty for being exhausted and needing some downtime. She saw it as selfish. I told her that taking care of herself is not selfish. It is self-full.

Just as filling yourself up with positive thoughts will eventually allow you to give that positivity away to others, self-care fills you and allows you to have more to give to others when they need it. By constantly giving in a relationship, you slowly grind that relationship down. By practicing self-care, you build it up.

She began to slowly dedicate thirty minutes a day to resting, reading, exercising, or chatting with a friend; since then, she feels refreshed and is enjoying her relationships with her husband and kids more. She has gone back to being joyful at spending time with her family rather than being resentful and feeling guilty that she couldn't give them more of herself.

If we wear ourselves out, we will not enjoy any part of our lives—even our favorite parts. My entire life, my mother tried to operate on empty—she was constantly drained and exhausted. She had so many stressors and responsibilities that she never did anything for herself. I believe that if she had, she would have been a more present mother.

Self-care changes you. By taking care of yourself, you are telling yourself you have value. And if you believe it, other people will believe it too, and they will know you deserve to be treated well. You are worth a dark chocolate Hershey's kiss and a bubble bath. You deserve to celebrate your own life! Each day is worth it. Enjoy!

The most effective way to see changes in your life is to implement a small bit of self-care.

Some ideas that take ten minutes or less:
- Drink more water. Aim for drinking half of your body weight in ounces every day. If you weigh 100 lbs., drink 50 oz. of water.
- Take supplements. At minimum, take a multi-vitamin, fish oil, and a probiotic.
- Schedule time to get together with or call a friend, even if it's only once a month.
- Wash your face and brush your teeth before bed. A warm washcloth can wash away stress from the day.
- Floss. You need your teeth to enjoy chocolate and smile!
- Make the perfect cup of coffee or tea and drink it slowly. Take time to inhale the aroma.

- Sleep on fresh sheets. At least once in a while, it feels good to crawl into a cozy bed.
- Read for ten minutes before bed or choose something uplifting to do first thing in the morning.
- Listen to your favorite radio station in the car, and sing like the rockstar you really are!
- Wear your favorite outfit. It will make you feel good and stand taller!
- Pet an animal or snuggle for a while.
- Meditate for five minutes when you feel stress taking over.
- Stretch your body as soon as you wake up. Just three seconds can change your day.
- Carry snacks in your bag to eat throughout the day. Try small munchies—nuts, bars, and fruit.
- Read a devotional. Be inspired! Set your mind on the good stuff!
- Keep a gratitude journal—record three things a day you're happy about and grateful for!
- Journal about three things you were able to give away.

After you work some easier bits of self-care into your day, try these strategies that take a little more time:
- Take a nap. Even ten or twenty minutes of closed eyes will do your body good.

- Sleep six or more hours a night, and create a bedtime routine.
- Move your body for at least twenty minutes a day. Get the heart pumping!
- Plan your meals for the week and grocery shop for them. Saturday and Sunday are great days for this!
- Take a class on something you've always wanted to try. Cook, dance, learn an instrument, or take a language class.
- Schedule time for work, play, rest, and meals. I like to set a timer for twenty minutes of *focus* and then five minutes to be distracted, then another twenty minutes of focus when I'm working for myself at home.
- Read a book—to learn, to enjoy, or to just be inspired!
- Have an in-depth discussion with a friend or partner. It might be a good idea to have a check-in time daily!
- Watch a favorite episode of TV. I love the ideas on *Shark Tank*.
- Get into nature. Walk, sit, rest, or read outside!
- Get a massage, a pedicure, a manicure, or a haircut. Spa time!
- Release built-up stress by doing yoga, Zumba, kickboxing, or running. Be sure to practice deep breathing.

Which of these can you pick to start today? Do one at a time—you don't need more on your to-do list—and use the time to enjoy yourself and just BE!

The most important thing to remember with self-care is that slow and steady wins the race. Self-care is meant to lighten your guilt and stress. Committing to too much self-care daily and then letting it fall by the wayside is only going to add to your worries, stress, and guilt. Remember to focus on making small strides each day.

One of my clients ran several medical clinics. She had a high-stress, time-sensitive job, and she came to me to find life-work balance and ease stress at home and work.

She was concerned that she wasn't living an exceptional life, and that managing hundreds of people at work and being a mother and wife pulled her in a million directions at once. So I asked her what change she could make to reduce her stress level in the coming week. She said she would work out four times that week; but when I asked her if that was something she wanted to do, she said no.

What about working out two times a week? She also didn't want to do that. It would just add more stress, trying to find the time to work that in. Then she said to me, "Do you know what I really want to do? This week I want to organize my closet. It's packed full with every season of clothing and most of it doesn't fit anymore. Every morning, I spend forty minutes trying to find a good outfit."

When she allowed herself to take into account what she wanted—without considering anyone else's needs—it was that easy for her to find her self-care activity.

She returned a week later and couldn't wait to check in. She had gone home, organized her closet by season, and gotten rid of nine bags of clothes. I congratulated her, but she wasn't finished: because she was able to get dressed so quickly, she had extra time in the morning and was able to work out twice!

She built a larger success off of a tiny change, creating the time and momentum necessary to move on and be more successful in the area of physical health.

Self-care takes commitment. It isn't always going to be easy to find the time, and sometimes you may not even feel like giving yourself that care. But keep in mind that once you feel comfortable in your skin, your life will feel more comfortable around you. Feel free to advocate for yourself and for your time to recharge. Your spouse can help by tweaking his or her schedule to help out, whether it be cooking dinner a few times a week or taking the kids out so you can have the house to yourself for a couple of hours. You can teach your kids to value you as a person rather than just a caretaker. Give yourself a time out, and let them know why. Set boundaries and limits for your kids so they know what you need, just as you know what they need. You may feel like you're neglecting to spend time with them, but spending two hours fully engaged with them is much better than three hours where you're barely keeping up with them.

> "A LOT OF PEOPLE ARE AFRAID TO SAY
> WHAT THEY WANT. THAT'S WHY THEY
> DON'T GET WHAT THEY WANT."
> —MADONNA

Give yourself permission to let a few things slide in honor of being happier. Maybe instead of vacuuming, you read. That's okay. Plan breaks in advance. Even if it's two years from now, working toward that vacation will give you motivation to power through the tougher days. If watching the news casts a gloomy cloud over your morning, turn the news off. Revel in the silence instead. You don't have to be up-to-date on everything that's happening if it's going to have negative repercussions on your whole day. You can wait until something positive has happened to take that on.

It is amazing to me what a different perspective people can have when they start to take care of themselves. A woman I was coaching once came to me and asked my opinion on a matter that was troubling her. She was bipolar and had been telling her three- and five-year-old daughters that her medication was just a vitamin. She was worried what they would think of her as they got older and learned that she was sick. Would they think she was a bad person for needing to be on medication?

I shook my head and said no. The fact that she was taking care of herself was beautiful. She was practicing the kind of self-care necessary to be the person her daughters needed her to be. Once they learned she was taking care of herself, they too would learn to love themselves. If my mother had taken care of herself in such a way, my life would have been very, very different.

Someone who is practicing self-care is happier, more relaxed, more patient, and even kinder. Life is busy, and it is easy for any of us to feel overwhelmed for a day, or even just a moment and take it out on someone else.

Once you begin to practice self-care, you can begin to recognize those around you who are overwhelmed and are lashing out as a result. Take a moment to remind them that they matter. Give an honest compliment. Respond kindly to rude people. Smile at someone frowning. Listen when someone talks. Ask how they are. Let someone merge ahead of you during rush hour. Look people in the eye. Thank them by name.

Soon, your positivity will cycle to include others and will return back to you. It will be a natural part of who you are.

In practicing healthful habits and self-care, I like to give people five tools to help them maintain their new lifestyle and keep them filled and joyful. I call these tools CANES because they are walking sticks, supporting roles, for your journey.

Commitment and Consistency

Being committed is about being 80 percent invested and then taking one more step forward. It is still showing up when other people are canceling, or when it is cold out and you don't feel like going. It is about pushing through a workout you don't want to do. It is about investing in yourself with a gym membership, a life coach, or more time for self-care. Commitment is caring about your own health—physical and mental—before you take care of everyone else's and understanding that taking care of yourself will make your relationships, health, and mindset better.

But it's important to remember that commitment alone isn't enough to stay healthy. Most people are committed to something very strongly on Monday, a little less on Tuesday, and then not at all on Wednesday. This is where consistency comes in!

It takes sixty-four days to change a habit, but not everything you do needs to be a forever commitment. I like to do thirty-day challenges to prove to myself that I can be committed *and* consistent for at least a few weeks. One month I might challenge myself to move every day for thirty minutes in a row. Or I might skip dessert for a month or stop drinking alcohol. What could you challenge yourself with to strengthen your ability to commit by being consistent?

Accountability and Action

This is what forces you to stay committed. We all need support and encouragement in our lives, people whom we can count on to be there and bring us up when we are down.

Ideal accountability partners (or accountabili-buddies) are there for you on your good days and the days you struggle. They celebrate with you when you do well and cheer you on when you fall behind. They never shame you. They always remind you that tomorrow will be better.

They are the friends who meet you for a workout, a walk, or a dance class instead of breakfast, lunch, happy hour, or dinner. Often, as a society, emphasis is placed on social gatherings surrounding food and drink and little movement instead of on activities that invigorate our bodies and minds. A fabulous choice for an accountability partner is someone who lives close by and can meet with you regularly, but that doesn't mean someone who lives farther and can only meet weekly can't be a great source of inspiration, as well.

Ask a friend to be your accountabili-buddy by trying something new with you—whether a class, a 5K, or a bike ride. Have one buddy or many—they'll get just as much out of it as you will!

Nutrition

Eating enough of the good stuff can be overwhelming: every day a new study comes out on what to eat, how much to eat, and what time of day to eat it.

I like to teach people to take back their power from

food—to not let food consume their lives or think of a food as inherently bad. Focus on portion control over restriction. If you don't think of foods as off limits, it'll be easier to say no! Restriction creates focus on what you can't have. Availability takes that focus away, empowering you to make good choices.

Eat a rainbow of color every day. Add fruits and vegetables for diversity, taste, and creativity. Did you know our taste buds change every six weeks? When was the last time you tried a new food?

If you have a family, let the kids pick a color and a corresponding food to try. On Mondays, try eating a red food. On Tuesdays, blue. Teach your kids about good food choices by involving them in meal planning and cooking. For example, on Thanksgiving, my oldest son gets to try a fun, experimental recipe with turkey; my daughter creates a new side dish for us; and my youngest is in charge of the potatoes.

Exercise

Exercise doesn't have to mean a workout . . . in fact, nothing about WORKout sounds fun—and I say that even though I own a gym! When we were kids, no one said, "Go work out," they said, "Go play." When was the last time you played? Do you even remember how to play? Kids play soccer and kickball and dance, jump rope, and skate. If we just move our bodies every day, not because we have to but because we want to, we will feel better emotionally and physically. Sometimes it is about running the laundry up and down the stairs to get my body moving; other days I am so busy all I can do is circle the kitchen counter three times. There is no wrong way to move your body—just move it every day. I have a girlfriend I love to meet at the mall to simply walk and talk together. We just chat it up, and in no time we've gotten four miles in. When was the last time you played? Walked the dog? Danced?

Supplementation, Stress, Sleep, and Success

Supplementation: I've worked with thousands of clients over the years, and I've heard the same concern from many of them: "I want to get healthy, but I want to do it the *natural* way." As in, the way without any dietary supplements. I understand and applaud the commitment to not taking shortcuts, but the truth is that supplements provide nutrients that can be very difficult—and very expensive—to get enough of. Portion control during meals and eating a variety of fruits and veggies can get you most of the way, but that isn't always going to get you the results that you want. Supplements fill in the cracks and help your body perform at its best. I use AdvoCare supplements, but there are dozens of good brands out there.

For most people, only taking a couple supplements will do the trick, so long as they are high quality. For people who are new to supplements, I advise you start with these three: a multi-vitamin that you can dissolve with a glass of water and take halfway through a meal; a quality fish oil supplement that you take at the same time as the multi-vitamin; and a probiotic that you take first thing in the morning on an empty stomach.

Stress: We all have some stress in our lives—I think that even on a tropical island you might burn one day and feel a little stressed—but it is how we manage our stress that counts. Do we conquer it, or does it eat away at us and constantly make us anxious? A kickboxing class is a great way to release stress. Journaling, talking, and walking it out are all great stress relievers. When you try to hold it all in and act as though nothing is wrong, stress causes the most damage to our physical health.

Things can be especially difficult to manage if we have multiple stressors coming at us at once, which is why it's especially important to look at how we can get more downtime, rest, relax, and reflect on what we can and cannot change before our lives become completely full of stress. Not only does this provide a ready-made game plan in tumultuous times, but it can proactively help us reduce stress as well. I like to use the Serenity

Prayer when stressors start to nag at me. It helps me embrace change as a way to let go of stressors, whether it be changing jobs, relationships, or locations. It can be easy to get caught up in the to-do list and forget that this change is for the better, and that I'm blessed to have the ability to make this change in my life—the Serenity Prayer acts as a reminder for me.

Here it is:
God, grant me the serenity
To accept the things I cannot change,
The courage to change the things I can,
And the wisdom to know the difference.

Follow the words of the Serenity Prayer and practice self-care—allow yourself more downtime, take naps, get a massage, go for a walk, or drink a glass of wine. All of these little things add up to reduce the amount of stress in your life. After all, you're much better equipped to take care of the tasks causing stress when you're healthy, mentally and physically.

Sleep: Getting enough sleep and the right kind of sleep is vital to staying healthy. When you are worn down, you are much more likely to get sick and much less likely to be engaged with what's going on around you. When it comes to sleep, routines will go far in making sure you fall asleep quickly and stay asleep. I like to take a hot shower or bath before bed—it helps me relax. If you need to settle your mind, try journaling about your day, praying, reading, or talking to a loved one on the phone. If your body is still restless at night, you can make your room more comfortable by spraying your pillow with lavender or turning on relaxing music or sounds before you go to bed.

Head to bed at the same time every night, and when you wake up, slowly stretch before you get out of bed. Be thankful for a new day, and start your morning routine slowly and deliberately. Giving your body adequate time to wake up will help invigorate your mind and give you a jump-start on your day.

Add some vital nutrients and stress-relieving exercises to your new routines, and you'll find yourself much more equipped to achieve that final S—the success you deserve!

To get started on your self-full journey, fill in the following:

I am happy when I _____

I feel refreshed when I _____

This week, I want to try _____

I will commit to _____

_____ for thirty days.

_____ is my accountability partner.

I need to take action in this part of my life: _____

_____

Foods I need to add to make sure I eat the whole rainbow:

_____

The next foods I will try: _____

I overeat when: _____

I will stop overeating by (eating from a smaller plate,

packing my lunch, etc.) _____

_____

A fun way for me to get exercise is by _____

_____

STEP 4

Be Flexible

"STEP OUT OF THE HISTORY THAT IS HOLDING
YOU BACK. STEP INTO THE NEW STORY
YOU ARE WILLING TO CREATE."
—OPRAH WINFREY

From ages eleven to thirteen, I weighed about sixty-eight pounds. I became obsessed with my body as a teenager—not the look of it, but its size. I felt insignificant and wanted to take up less space. At nineteen, I ended up in the hospital under constant supervision. I was losing weight even though I was pregnant.

Struggling with anorexia is not about food; it is about giving yourself power over your own life when everything around you is outside of your control. It is a coping mechanism for when the world gets too overwhelming. In my turbulent life, my body was the one thing I could control to the extreme. It didn't help that my looks and my body were the only things I thought I had to offer the world. When I was about four, I remember my dad telling me I was sexy for the first time, and it continued after that. One of my older sisters would say, "How come everyone thinks you're the pretty one?" When I was really little, the attention was flattering; but as I got older, I realized the message I really heard was, "You are not smart, strong, or capable. All you have to offer this world is your looks." I never felt pretty, but being sexy was all I thought I could do. It was the only way I knew how to get something or to be seen.

Now, I always have bowls of little snacks on the counter. I offer food to every person who comes into my home. It's my new tradition, a part of my healing journey—I want people to know that my home is a safe place, that there is food and support and a community for everyone. Growing up with the insecurity of not having enough food and then suffering from an eating disorder made food a trigger for me, a source of conflict and stress in my life, and my new habit takes that association away and makes it positive instead. It allows me to take command over my past demons by turning them into angels for others.

Another way I take the pain of my childhood and turn it into something positive is by opening my home. I have lived in the same house now for twenty years, which is much longer than I have ever lived anywhere. I wanted nothing more in this world than to make my children feel secure, like they had a home, and that included making sure their friends felt like that as well. My sons' friends learned that my door was always open, and they were always welcome. It didn't matter if it was the middle of the night or Thanksgiving dinner. I've had people come and stay for the afternoon, one night, or even three months.

One night, when I was in the midst of hosting a get-together with some friends, my front door opened and a teenaged boy walked in, got something to eat, and sat down at the computer. My guests were shocked. "A strange boy just came into the house!" they said. I just smiled. The boy was my son's friend. He was going to college locally and needed a quiet place to write a paper for class.

It might not seem like much, but after spending most of my life on unsteady feet, it overjoys me that I have the privilege of providing the resources of a home, food, and a listening ear to everyone around me. But it's more than that. I am now living my life the way I want to be. I am not letting my past dictate the way I live my life today. I am acknowledging the truth of what happened to me, yes, but I am making conscious choices to create habits and traditions that break the cycle of my past, not continue it.

Sometimes, breaking cycles isn't just about changing what you *do*. It can be about changing how you *think*. During one of the dumpster-diving missions my siblings and I went on as children, we came across hundreds of angel food cakes, which we ate until the very taste of them made us sick. We had plenty left, so we decided to sell them on the street corner in order to buy other snacks; but as we were doing so, a police officer came by and told us we had to stop because we were selling stolen food. I was shocked—I had never thought of what we were doing as stealing. In my mind, we were just surviving. This was a pivotal moment for me—the moment the shame started.

For twenty years, I managed to avoid eating angel food cake. The association was just too much for me. But when I met my husband, wouldn't you know, his family loved angel food cake. They ate it for every holiday, get-together, and celebration, and they continue to do so to this day. I didn't have the heart to tell them about my experience, as angel food cake is my father-in-law's favorite dessert, so I would grin and bear it, keeping my memories to myself.

But a few months ago, as I was praying at church about some childhood wounds I wanted to let go of, this story came up, and I divulged it to my prayer partner. She listened carefully, then looked at me and said, "You know, you could have found rolls, cupcakes, or bread, but you didn't. You found angel food cake. Don't you get it? God met you there; he provided 200 angels and manna from heaven. Though it was not filled with protein and vitamins, it provided for you and your family in your great time of need."

In that moment, her words helped shift my perspective, not just of that particular story, but of my childhood situation in general. I began to focus on what I had been given, rather than what I had lacked as a child. Suddenly, I wasn't embarrassed anymore about the run-in with the police. I was thankful that for all those weeks I had something to eat instead of going hungry, as so many other people do. All it took was a little help from a devoted friend and a willingness to be open-minded.

What story in your life needs a little shift in perspective? Could you look at something with new eyes and see it in a new, positive way? It can be easy to become attached to a certain way of thinking, to take comfort in the idea of yourself as a victim of a situation. But if you continue to do that, you will only allow the situation to have power over you. To truly take ownership of your past, you must reconcile with it and be able to look at it in a positive light, possibly even going so far as to benefit others with what you've learned from your experiences.

If you want to be the Exception, you must turn your excuses into empowerment, from *why* something won't ever work to why you will make it work. If your family has always been overweight and struggles with diabetes, dedicate yourself to being physically healthy instead of giving in to what you consider to be the inevitable. Say to yourself, *"Because my family has struggled with weight issues for generations, I will do everything it takes to remain healthy and fit."*

Because of my history with food, I like to do short challenges to break any bad cycles I might be creating without knowing it. For three weeks, I'll drink a protein shake every day. For three weeks, I'll plan all of my meals. Three weeks is the sweet timeframe because three weeks is the amount of time it takes to instill a new idea or break a bad habit. What can be your three-week challenge?

You don't have to wait to change things—to break a cycle or build a tradition. Decide today that you're going to look at the As on your child's report card before the Fs. That you're going to give a compliment before you criticize yourself or someone else. That you will make a holiday or birthday happy and supportive, rather than tense and stressful. Albert Einstein said the definition of insanity is doing the same thing over and over and expecting different results. He was right. If you need change in your life, start by creating a healthy, positive new trend or tradition that eradicates an old, destructive one.

> "I CHOOSE TO MAKE THE REST OF MY LIFE
> THE BEST OF MY LIFE."
> —LOUISE HAY

Some people don't believe they have choices, but I have yet to hear of a situation that doesn't have at least two options. I know a woman who inherited the BRCA1 gene, which almost certainly causes breast cancer. Most of the women in her family had died of cancer, and it seemed inevitable that she would follow suit. But she realized that she had a choice—she might still develop breast cancer somewhere down the line, but she could take the necessary steps to reduce her risk. It was not an easy decision, but she decided to have a double mastectomy and hysterectomy. Emotionally and physically, her journey was very difficult—she faced long, painful, wearing hours in the hospital. But that struggle allowed her to be a part of her children's lives for longer than her own mother had been a part of her life.

For that woman, the decision was whether or not to allow a prescribed condition to control her. What I see more often than that are people who have to make the choice of whether or not to let another person control them. I had a client a while ago who was convinced she was stuck in her situation. Her husband was emotionally abusive and unfaithful, but she felt she needed his income to survive, so she stayed. She was understandably afraid of him and what would happen if she tried to change her situation, so much so that she shied away from the choices that were in front of her—but they were still there. She had at least three choices: to stay and act like she was okay, to seek help through counseling to work on their marriage, or to leave and find another way to survive.

Sometimes cycles repeat themselves so many times we think this is how it always has been and how it always will be. Breaking a cycle isn't easy, and it takes hard work, but it *is always possible*. **The options in front of you aren't always preferable or easy, but they're *always there*.**

When we feel like someone is making us do something, it is because we have given that person our power. We have forgotten that, ultimately, we decide how we will allow ourselves to be treated. When we think we are not worth speaking up for, or taking care of, we give others permission to treat us poorly. We might not always control what happens to us, but we do control how we respond. I use past abuse and betrayal as fuel to make me stronger and move me forward.

Of course, for some of us, the idea that we have control might be too large to grasp all at once. I understand that—there are certainly times in my life when I would have scoffed at the idea that I was stronger than my surroundings, which is why I suggest starting out small.

I have a client who struggles with depression and is bipolar. If you have ever suffered from depression—whether temporary or more long-term—you know that one misfortune can spiral and snowball until everything turns black, and there are days, weeks, entire months when finding just one bright spot in the day feels nearly impossible. This client continually focuses on how he never does anything right or finishes anything. To this client, the idea of being a failure overwhelms any hope to the contrary.

On top of him taking his medication, I gave him a simple task to start breaking the cycle of beating himself down and thinking of himself as a failure. I told him to start small with making simple, stabilizing choices—specifically, I told him to start making his bed each morning. It might seem silly, but for those of us who grew up with instability, unpredictability, and chaos, it is a beautiful and simple way to feel a little more in control and successful. And that one success is the stepping-stone to larger successes.

Making your bed is just one of a variety of simple, clear reminders that each day you have a clean slate to make good decisions. That you can choose what you are going to make of each new sunrise. Even if your week has consisted of a pattern of poor choices, today can be different.

Tell yourself these things:
- I will not allow myself to fall back into a dysfunctional or unhealthy life.
- I am strong enough to take that first step forward.
- I can decide to do the right thing because I decide what's best for myself.
- I don't need someone else to validate my choices—believing in myself is enough.
- I can break my pattern of poor choices.
- I am bigger than my surroundings.
- I have power over my past.

To help you believe in yourself, write an affirmation or read an inspiring quote. I love Marianne Williamson's quote, **"Our deepest fear is not that we are inadequate. Our deepest fear is that we are powerful beyond measure."**

Keep in mind that it's okay to make mistakes and slip into old patterns once in a while. It'll take some work to break old habits completely, and if you're too hard on yourself, you're liable to quit altogether. It's also important to recognize that you might never be 100 percent happy with where you are in a new cycle, and that's a good thing! It'll keep you striving and improving every day!

It will also help you recognize when others are caught up in their own cycles. A number of years ago, I was hired by a non-profit to speak on its behalf to companies all over the Twin Cities. When the day came, I was nervous but excited. I got started with my speech and thought it was going well, but as I was talking, I saw the organizer walk out of the room. It was distracting, but I shook it off and didn't think about it again until the day before the second speech at that organization.

When I called the organizer to finalize the details of my second speech, she cut me off and told me she didn't want me to come back. I was shocked and a little put off. After I hung up, I called the company who had set up the event, and told the supervisor that the organizer didn't want me to come back. My supervisor said I needed to go and share my story, even though I wasn't wanted.

When I called the organizer to tell her that I would be speaking, she demanded that if I had to come, she didn't want me to speak. You see, there was another man coming and she wanted him to speak instead. Now at this point, I was tempted to lose my temper and let her know explicitly just how I felt about the situation.

But I held my tongue and instead thought about what else might be going on. Had I done something to offend this lady? Had I been unprofessional? Had there been a mixup on my part? I was hurt by the situation and by her demeanor, but I wasn't going to let it affect the opportunity I had to go and speak; I was asked to do a professional job, and I was committed to doing it!

The next morning, as I was standing with and getting to know the other speaker, the organizer came over to us and let me know that the other speaker was to have ten minutes to talk, and I was going to have only two. The other speaker, though, had heard about me and my story and told the organizer that I had to speak longer. I just stood there, uncomfortable. Once again, I was frustrated and a bit embarrassed, but the organizer gave in and allowed me more time to speak.

I was planning on telling the story about being forced to move out of my house as a teenager, and it's a difficult one to share. She offered us breakfast, and at this point, my stomach was stirring, and I was nervous. I was nervous and had to physically and emotionally psych myself up to share the story. Speaking never makes me nervous, but rejection always reminds me of feeling abandoned by both of my parents, and that is what makes it difficult.

As I stood up there, I realized that it was the most difficult speech I had ever had to give. Talking about my past always makes me feel vulnerable, and I was already feeling wounded and unwanted because of this woman, just like I felt as a teenager in my story. But I kept reminding myself that I *wasn't* unwanted. I was worthy of the room's attention, and I was a good speaker. I broke the cycle of feeling unwanted and unworthy, and proved to myself that it didn't matter what she thought of me.

When I was done with my talk, I went to get more food. As I was standing at the food table, the organizer of the event approached me and again asked to speak with me. I was still ticked off with her, and all I wanted to do was scream, "NO!" at the top of my lungs. But instead I smiled and said sure, thinking that I wouldn't want someone to yell at me.

She told me she wanted to apologize for being so

rude, and that I didn't deserve that kind of treatment. She told me she'd been really stressed out and unhappy lately. During my first talk, she had to leave the room to take care of a family emergency, and when I called her to finalize the details of my presentation, she was in a fitting room trying to find something to wear for a wedding. She'd known about the wedding for nine months and kept putting off shopping because she had promised herself she would lose twenty pounds but hadn't done so and was upset with herself and the way she looked in every outfit she tried. To top it all off, she had been so busy with work that she hadn't had time for friends or even family, and she didn't really have any work friends because her field is so male-dominated, so she had been handling all of her stress by herself. She admitted that she had taken all of those negative feelings out on me and apologized once again.

I was overwhelmed by her apology. She had been caught in a cycle of negative self-talk, and I had just happened to catch her at a vulnerable time. When I realized how much she had been struggling with herself and her situation, it was easy for me to forgive her and have compassion for her struggles. The only reason I could do this, though, is because I too have been caught up in my own negative cycles and have had to break free. In times such as that, I am thankful for the obstacles that I have overcome in my life because they have better equipped me to understand other people's pain and to offer whatever I can to make their lives a bit easier.

One thing that really stuck with me after this encounter is how, even though the organizer was surrounded by people, she felt completely alone—and I realized how commonplace that is and how much harder it can make our lives. When we feel alone, we are subject to our own criticism—and it's definitely true that some of the harshest voices in our lives are from our own heads—but we've removed ourselves from our fans. Having that support system around to lean on when things get tough and to hold you accountable for following through with your resolutions is almost as important as making those resolutions in the first place.

Think about who makes up your fan base, then think about who else you can add to it. Do you only rely on people who are geographically close to you? Can you add in another friend or family member by having a weekly phone call? Are you as open with your best friend, significant other, or spouse as you could be? Is there a coworker, a friend of a friend, or someone in your workout class who you think would be fun to grab lunch with, but haven't approached yet? **It might be uncomfortable, but everyone needs friends and support groups, and you may be doing that person a favor as well as yourself.**

Once you have built a great support system, it's important to be intentional about keeping up with them. Remember that a support system works both ways—you have to give to one another. It can be tough to find the time, so getting something down as a repeated, scheduled event can be extremely helpful. A friend taught me once about a wonderful strategy that she uses to keep connected and open with her spouse. She said they get together every night for a glass of wine at nine p.m. and relax with one another. They have a set time to devote solely to one another, putting aside the stress of the day. They use this time to unwind together.

Now, this doesn't mean you have to drink a glass of wine every night, but it is important that you take a few minutes to be intentional about the time you spend with another person. Turn off your phones. Make sure you don't have any screens. Look each other in the eyes and share your day's successes, failures, and dreams. Feel free to whine at nine about your day, but move past it and make sure you focus on the good stuff, too. After all, that's what a good support system does—reminds you about all of the good present in your life.

> "IF YOU LOOK AT WHAT YOU HAVE IN LIFE,
> YOU'LL ALWAYS HAVE MORE. IF YOU LOOK
> AT WHAT YOU DON'T HAVE IN LIFE, YOU'LL
> NEVER HAVE ENOUGH."
> —OPRAH WINFREY

Extend this routine to your children—check in over breakfast or dinner. Extend it to your friends—schedule time weekly or monthly or even quarterly to connect. Life is busy, and it can be easy to take our relationships for granted. Don't let that happen. You never know when an important relationship might just be what changes, or saves, your life or someone else's.

And you never know where you might find truly great friends. Once, when I was running errands and found myself close to where a friend of mine lives, I decided to stop by to see if she was home. I rang the doorbell, and her husband answered. "She's not home," he said. "But thanks for coming over! I love that you didn't call before you stopped over!"

I thought he was being sarcastic. He wasn't.

He invited me in for coffee and sat me down and told me a story about his grandparents. They always had a pot of coffee on and the door open, just in case anyone wanted to stop by. He said he loved that tradition and that random visits really encouraged openness and honest connection. We ended up having a really lovely visit, even though I previously never would have considered going over there with the intent to see him as well as his wife. **You never know when and where you might find additions to your fan base, if only you keep an open mind.**

One of the most important parts of meeting with your fan base is that they get you out of your head for a little while. The cycle of self-negativity is so easy to fall into, and it can be difficult to pull yourself out. Meeting up with a friend and hearing them say, "That outfit is so cute!" "I'm so glad we met up—I've missed you!" or "Tell me about your new project—I bet you're killing it!" can help quiet that discouraging voice inside your head. Even seeing a friend smile at you can change your mood around completely.

This isn't to say the voice in your head is never going to go away. But it can stop being negative. If you work on it every day and if you allow yourself to be supported by people who love you, you can rewrite that destructive script running through your brain. It's not easy, but you can do it!

With my angel food cake story, it took a caring friend to make me change my perspective. I'd like to do that for you now. Instead of obsessing over the bad things going on, think about having a bed, a roof, food, a job, a healthy body, and people you love. Try writing these things down, making a habit of journaling what you're grateful for. Now write down three things you gave away or did for another person. Did you recently clean out your closet or storage space and donate to charity? Did you extend a smile and a genuine compliment to someone having a bad day? Did you help a friend work through something that has been bothering her? Did you suggest an idea that solved a problem at work? Taking stock of these things will help you realize just how much you have to offer.

Take this one step further and create belief cards or mantras you can revisit every day. Belief cards are just index cards (or pieces of paper) with a belief written on them that help you rewrite the story of who you are. Even if your whole childhood someone told you that you have no value and nothing to offer this world, even if you told yourself a million times you have nothing good inside you, the belief cards and mantras can start to enforce a new truth.

Begin with three to ten beliefs and add more over time! Read your cards in the morning, before bed—as many times per day as you need. Keep a stack by your bed, by your computer, at your desk. Whenever you find yourself slipping into self-criticism, negate those bad thoughts with a card.

Here are examples of what I have written on belief cards:

- I am smart
- I am a good singer
- I am stronger than I think
- I can finish what I start
- I am a writer
- I have value
- I could be a rock star
- I deserve healthy relationships
- I am beautiful
- I am capable
- I can overcome
- I was created for more
- I am worth unconditional love
- I am able to love unconditionally

Are you ready?
It's your turn:

I believe:

- I am able to transform my life

- I will be happy

- I will become _____

- I deserve _____

- I am capable of _____

- I feel _____

- _____

- _____

- _____

- _____

- _____

If it's too hard to write positively about yourself at first, look for quotes, poems, or stories instead. Read them until you start to believe them, until they are louder than all the negative voices in your head, until they make you smile. At first it will seem a little silly, uncomfortable, and maybe even disappointing. But if you stick with it, you'll start to see how those empowering words apply to you, and you will eventually begin to believe them.

STEP 5

Be Gentle

"It's one of the greatest gifts you can
give yourself, to forgive.
Forgive everybody."
—Maya Angelou

When you think of the word gentle, what comes to mind? Kittens, babies, soft blankets? What about being gentle with yourself?

There are many times in your life when circumstances are rough, and you might feel battered, broken, and ashamed for not making it through unscathed. These are the times when you have to find that softness within yourself, to help heal the wounds the world has left on you. This involves letting go of the harshness and looking on the world once again with gentle eyes.

I got one of my harshest wounds when I was sixteen. I worked as a live-in nanny over the summer for a family who owned a bar and restaurant. They paid me very well to care for their three children, as well as giving me gifts, taking me on nice vacations, and treating me like a member of their family. It had the potential to be one of the best summers of my life—until one night when the dad, who was like a father to me, took me to the bar he and his wife owned to show me around.

He gave me a Long Island Iced Tea, and then a few more. Once I was drunk, he took me to the lake by their house and told me we would go swimming. He raped me instead.

The next day, I was in shock from what had happened. While everyone was going about the day as usual—parents going to work, kids playing—I was broken, in emotional and physical pain, ashamed at myself for once again trusting someone only to be taken advantage of. When the mother returned home in the evening, the house was trashed. I hadn't been able to make myself clean up after the kids. The mother asked if something was wrong, and I said yes, but I could not bring myself to tell her what had happened. She told me to call my mom to sort out whatever was bothering me.

When I called my mom and told her I had been assaulted, I expected her to be my ally, to ask me to come back home and to tell me what I needed to do to feel better. To defend me, protect me, help me process. Instead, she said, "They pay well, and this is a job you need."

I had never felt more betrayed. As a mother, I would do anything for my kids. I'm even a bit overprotective if someone looks at them the wrong way or says something unkind—just the thought of someone taking advantage of my children, in any way, riles me up. But my mother weighed my pain and the potential for further suffering against my absence from the house and a steady paycheck, and she decided I should keep the job. She did nothing, was unable to offer even the slightest comfort. Her response was a difficult thing to forgive.

Against my mother's wishes, I ended up leaving that job with the family. It was too hard to be around not only the father but the family that he had betrayed when he forced himself on me. I moved in with one of my older sisters. The pain of that horrible night haunted me— enough that one night I took an entire bottle of sleeping pills and washed them down with a bottle of vodka. My sister came home, found me passed out, and called 911. I ended up in ICU with my stomach pumped. I remember waking up to my older sister brushing the chunks of thrown-up charcoal out of my hair.

From there, I was sent to a treatment facility to deal with my addiction problems, but my addiction wasn't the problem. It was the result. I had been violated and felt hopeless and lonely, like I was in a deep, dark hole, with no hope, and no light. At the time, I didn't understand it well enough to classify myself as severely depressed, but by age sixteen, I had already been through so much trauma that I really did not want to go on living. I could not take the pain anymore.

I was so angry at my mother and my rapist, I was suffocated by resentment. But after I ended up in the hospital, I realized that refusing to let go of the pain would literally kill me.

Letting go of that pain and anger was a process and a difficult decision. I'll never forget the wrong they both did to me, but instead of staying angry and letting that anger control my life, I chose and continue to choose to use my experience as a way to reach out and help others. I cannot change my past, so instead I focus on changing my future.

This step—being gentle—is about opening yourself up

enough to let go of all the terrible, difficult things in your past that are holding you down.

Being gentle is about being vulnerable. Freeing yourself from your past cannot be done with force—it only happens when you accept that you can't change your past. Gentleness is about knowing and naming the hurt in your soul, embracing it, and, in that same breath, removing the power it has over you.

Similar to letting go of grief, letting go of your past and moving on is a process; and just as there are six steps to grieving, there are steps and benchmarks in this process as well. I call them the four Fs: **failure, faith, forgiveness, and freedom.**

Failure

You might think you can avoid traditional ideas of failure on your journey to living a better life, but you can't. In fact, you should even look forward to failing. When we encounter failure, we encounter priceless opportunities to learn, grow, and develop ourselves into a closer version of who we'd like to become. When we learn to fail, we can relax and not worry so much about being perfect or doing everything correctly the first time. We can quit holding ourselves to such high standards and take a leap of faith. There is freedom in giving yourself permission to try something you would traditionally shy away from.

Many of my clients struggle with perfectionism, and it becomes the norm for them to go to bed frustrated about the areas where they believe they fall short. I tell them to allow themselves a little grace. Instead of focusing on where they missed the mark, I ask them what they can learn from their failure and how they can improve because of it.

I focus on driving home this point: you are not a failure because you experience failure. You are human, a work in process, and no one is perfect, even though some pretend to be.

I like to say if I don't get told "no" ten times a day, I'm not asking enough questions or taking enough risks. In sales, you have to plan on being rejected. I love the SW rule: Some Will, Some Won't. So What? Someone is Waiting. If someone turns me down in my life or business, that's okay. Getting told no does not make you a failure and does not define who you are.

Being told no is scary, but it's also an indicator that I'm pushing myself. There's a good chance that if the only response you get is "yes," you are waiting too long, playing it too safe, and not growing as much as you could be. The more you're told no, the easier it will become, and you'll realize that failure isn't as scary anymore.

"COURAGE IS LIKE A MUSCLE.
WE STRENGTHEN IT BY USE."
—RUTH GORDON

Know that as you fail, you might disappoint yourself and other people. But not as much as you would if you quit striving for growth. If you ask for grace, for support, and for forgiveness, you'll be surprised at how often you'll get those things. There's a good chance that your support network is growing, too, and needs you to promise to give grace, support, and forgiveness right back. So keep pushing and striving for greatness; if you believe in yourself, you will grow more than you ever thought possible.

Faith

After you've accepted—and maybe even welcomed—that you will fail, begin to focus on your faith. Who or what do you have faith in? The obvious answer here is a higher power, but your answer doesn't have to be spiritual—your faith can lie in God but can also lie in your support system: a mentor, coach, family member, trainer, or support group.

If you do practice a religion and put faith in a religious authority, it is important to remember what it is that your religion is preaching—to be gentle and kind to yourself and those around you.

A few years ago, I was invited to attend a talk a friend of mine was giving, and before the speech there was a happy hour. I invited a friend of mine—a conservative Christian—to join me. When we got to the happy hour, we were joined by a large group of women my friend and I wouldn't normally spend time with together. One of the women was telling us her entire life story, talking about how she had been married and divorced three times, and how her sixteen-year-old daughter was sent to live with her second husband. She was depressed, alone, and unhappy, and to make matters worse, her birthday was that week, and she was going to spend it alone.

Another woman overheard and started to cry. It was her birthday as well, and she, a hoarder and a single mom with four kids, also felt alone. I was overcome with compassion and empathy for both of their situations, having had similar experiences.

I went to the bar and asked if they did anything for birthdays (they gave free ice cream!). A few minutes later, a waiter brought out two plates of dessert and a stack of spoons, and we all celebrated these women's birthdays with them. They both gave everyone huge hugs and said it was the nicest thing anyone has ever done for them— even though it didn't cost me anything except a moment of my time.

On the way home, my friend turned to me and said I had taught her a valuable lesson—for all of her life, she tried to be a good Christian in that she went to church every Sunday, prayed, and said grace. But watching my kindness toward those women, not judging them, but instead celebrating them when no one else would, was really something Jesus would do. She resolved to pay more attention to what her faith was really telling her and to be gentle with others in the way she was taught.

No matter how important your religious authority is to you—whether God is the most important thing or not important at all—there is one other person you need to have faith in: yourself.

If you don't have faith in yourself, you constantly doubt your actions; if you constantly doubt your actions, you cannot confidently create change. In 2007, I bought my first Snap Fitness franchise. The day my husband and I closed on it, the previous owner said something to me that felt like a punch to the gut. We had just signed the paperwork and were walking out of the lawyer's office when he turned to me and said in a sarcastic voice, "Just so you know, I have been bleeding money for three months, and now I am hemorrhaging. Good luck to you!"

My belly hit the floor. I was already nervous about running the business full time, and I knew it had been struggling a bit. The gym was in a small town about forty-five minutes south of where my husband and I live, and I didn't know the community very well. The venture could very easily have failed.

But I had faith in myself and my abilities as a business owner, and the seller's taunt just fueled my drive for success, sparked my "just watch me" attitude. You see, people have been telling me my whole life that things won't work out, and I've always done my best to prove them wrong.

I met every neighbor, knocked on doors, partnered with other businesses, and joined the Chamber of Commerce and the Rotary Club. Four months later, we were ranked number four in the nation for new Snap Fitness members, and corporate called me to train new potential Snap Fitness owners.

While the most important thing is to have faith in yourself, it's also important to remember that you can't only rely on and have faith in yourself—that's too much pressure to take care of everything alone. I have faith in myself, but I also have faith that God, my friends, my mentors, my family, and others will tell me the truth, hold me accountable, encourage me when I need it, and support me on my journey. I have faith that I can count on them.

In times of failure, you need faith to move you forward from struggle to success. Having many shoulders to lean on eases the burden. If you're having trouble moving on because you're not quite big enough for it, having faith in and the faith of others will allow you to go farther than you would on your own. I take comfort in **Jeremiah 29:11: "For I know the plans I have for you," declares the Lord, "plans to prosper you and not to harm you, plans to give you hope and a future."** What do you take comfort in?

Forgiveness

Forgiveness is the hardest, longest step of the letting go process. It is in forgiveness that we are finally able to move beyond our past mistakes or hurts and begin to move forward in freedom. Without forgiveness we can and will get stuck in our own muck. **Forgiveness is larger than yourself and your feelings. It is what allows you to step up and do the right thing.**

I was a single mother and my first son was six months old when I got pregnant for the second time. When I found out, I felt like I had been given a death sentence. I was broke and tired, and I could barely provide for one baby, much less two.

My sister, four years older than me, had always wanted a baby but didn't have any kids. She offered to adopt my second baby, Emily, and took her home from the hospital right after she was born.

Being a birth mother, a mother who places her child up for adoption, isn't different than being any other kind of mother as far as your heart is concerned. You don't love your child any less because you chose someone else to raise your child. Sometimes I think you have *to love them more* in order to let them go.

At first, adoption seemed like an answer to my prayer, but soon I began to obsess over whether or not I made the right decision. Early on in the adoption process, I began to change my mind. I knew it wouldn't be fair to my sister, but what about me? Or this baby? Would I be giving her a better life or a worse one by giving her up?

For years it was very hard to be around my sister's family and hear Emily call my sister "Mom." It ripped out my heart. When Emily was two years old, they moved to another state. I thought a family adoption would be good so I could still be part of Emily's life, but it was not meant to be, and I didn't see her grow up. They visited once or twice a year, but I missed most of her childhood.

Some people who have had experience with adoption say it was the greatest thing in their life. Others consider it a tragedy. In my case, it was both. I experienced the shame of being an unwed mother, buried in guilt and embarrassment and judged by others to be a failure; unworthy. To carry a baby is uncomfortable. It stretches your physical body and makes you sick. I delivered Emily without medicine, filled with pain, and watched as a part of my body was taken from me. I cried myself to sleep for weeks for the loss of her. The only thing that got me through was that my sister would give her more than I could.

Today, Emily is getting her master's degree and is a successful, bright, kind, lovely woman. Her adoption was a gift because it allowed her to be the person she is today. It was the right choice. But even though my head knows that, my heart didn't always agree.

I felt for years that I had done something wrong and that I needed to be absolved. And I did. I needed to forgive myself for making the hardest decision in the world. Because even though I was the best mother I could be, I blamed myself for not being enough. It was only through forgiving myself that I was able to have a relationship with Emily. In acknowledging that I did the best I could, I was able to be who I was with her, and we could both be free of regret and pain that came from a difficult situation.

Everyone has different situations that lead to giving a child up for adoption and different reasons for doing so.

I grew up feeling abandoned and neglected, and I never wanted my kids to feel that, even if it meant I couldn't be their mom. I know intimately the harm of having an absent mother. Whatever your situation and reason, it's important to remember that adoption is never abandonment. It is a hope and a prayer that someone else can give your child a better life and more time and love than you could. It is easy to reprimand yourself for being cruel; it takes courage to realize that keeping your child under detrimental circumstances is selfish.

Years ago, I knew another single mother like myself. We were not super close, but we were still friends. She didn't have a lot of family, but she was very close to a brother who was in the army. After getting off duty, he asked to stay with her. He had been living with her and her young son for a few weeks when her son told her that his uncle had played an icky game with him and had touched him in a way he did not like.

My friend was horrified, filled with pain, shame, and guilt. She thought she had been doing a good thing, offering her brother a place to stay while he got back on his feet after his time in the army, and yet she had failed as a mother and didn't protect her son.

She filed charges but still had to tell others in her family about it. When she told her family, she realized that many of them knew about her brother's past of hurting children, but never did anything to stop it. Eventually, the truth came out that he was AWOL and that he was also an addict. During the trial, I was the only person to sit on my friend's side of the courtroom. None of her family could admit what had happened.

Thankfully, the brother was put in jail and received treatment, but it was still hard for my friend—she couldn't stop blaming herself. She started working with a therapist, coach, and prayer mentor. They all emphasized that it was not her fault, that she couldn't have known what would happen, and eventually she was able to accept that as well through relying on her faith, knowing that God would forgive both her and the perpetrator. See, it was only when she forgave herself and gave herself permission to accept that she couldn't control everything that she could step up and support her healing child in the way he needed to get better.

If she hadn't accepted that what happened was terrible, and that she wasn't nor could ever be a perfect mom, she would have truly failed as a mother. Holding in anger and resentment will make you physically sick if you hold on to it long enough. Many people jump into addictive behaviors when they stay in anger and regret. Eventually, through prayer and support and the moving power of the Holy Spirit, my friend was able to forgive her brother. It may seem convoluted that she did so, but if she hadn't, she would have stayed so wrapped up in her own pain that she wouldn't have been able to focus on being the wonderful mother she is.

Unfortunately, I can't give you a magic set of steps on how to forgive yourself or someone else. It doesn't work the same for everyone. I can tell you, though, that there are many different layers to forgiveness. **You might find that forgiving others is easier than forgiving yourself. You are, after all, your biggest critic.**

If you make the same mistake again and again, like only eating fast food or dating the wrong guy, it's even harder to let it go. If you are constantly feeding the fire of your self-hatred, you won't ever be able to take the time to smother those mistakes and bad habits. Just as your past can't control your present and future, your anger can't control your behavior. If you solely focus on your flaws, you'll never be able to see your own strength; and if you can't see your own strength, you won't be able to work past your flaws. It is a vicious cycle.

Had I only focused on my perceived weakness at having to let Emily go, I never would have recognized the courage it took for me to offer her a better life, and I never would have been able to have the relationship with

Emily that I do now. Had my friend only focused on her perceived fault in the abuse of her son, she never would have been able to recognize the strength it took for her to intervene and stop that abuse—strength that no one else in her family had shown—and she would never have been able to give her son the support he needed.

It is important to recognize and take steps to redirect our flaws and bad habits, but it is even more important to constantly be aware of our own goodness and be okay with forgiving ourselves for the mistakes we make. It might take something silly, like a *Saturday Night Live*-like sketch, where you repeat, "I am good, I am nice, and by golly, people like me," to remind yourself daily that you are beautiful and strong and worth loving, but you must focus on doing so. Laugh at and with yourself until you learn to let go and love yourself in spite of your flaws and mistakes. Until you do so, you won't be able to achieve the final F.

Freedom

This is the Big F. **Freedom means having the ability to make it through the day with a real smile. It means being yourself, instead of someone you think you have to be. It means you show up and give all that you have and still continue to grow every day.**

Freedom is about experiencing joy and believing in

yourself and your dreams, rather than the negative voices around you and in your head.

I live free every day because I have nothing and no one holding me back. I have forgiven my mother for the hurt she caused me as a child. I understand that she did the best she could, even though it wasn't good enough, and that is enough for me now. I have forgiven myself for my past mistakes, for staying in dangerous situations, and for not standing up for myself or believing in myself as much as I could. I have no more bitterness about my past. I know I am doing everything I can to be the amazing woman that I am meant to be and to share everything I have to offer with those around me. I know that one good thing I do in the present outweighs multiple poor choices I made in the past.

"I DIDN'T GET THERE BY WISHING FOR IT OR HOPING FOR IT, BUT BY WORKING FOR IT."
—ESTÉE LAUDER

Every day, I take one more step toward my perfect life. I'll never be a perfect person, but I often fall off track and then hop back on without beating myself up too much. I cry when I need to, burn stress when I need to, and try to not let negativity carry across from day to day. Each morning is a clean slate.

Having a past of destructive behavior does not mean that you don't deserve true happiness today and in the future. Don't fuel your own demons. Your mistakes do not define you. My demons have been left in the past. I remember them—I'll never forget—but they are not part of me now. I have learned to accept and even embrace myself, including the messy parts. The good, the bad, and the ugly, it's all me, and I embrace it! **Now is your time to do the same.**

What steps will you take toward being free?

What does freedom look like to you? What does it feel like?

Use this tool to help discover what is keeping you from letting go:

I failed at _____

_____ but I am not a failure

I still blame _____ because

of _____

But I believe in _____

_____ and that will help me through

I haven't forgiven _____

I want to be free because_____

_____

Being free to me means_____

_____

I will let go of _____

_____

I will accept others'_____

_____

_____ even if I don't agree or understand

I am open to consider forgiving _____

_____

STEP 6

Be Courageous

"It takes as much energy to wish
as it does to plan."
—Eleanor Roosevelt

It takes courage to do many things in life. It is risky to start a new company, to ask for a sale, or to begin a new career. It is risky to start a new relationship, or try out a new workout routine. **But one of the most courageous things you can do is forgive.**

Forgiving is wise; forgiving and forgetting is not. Being able to acknowledge and reconcile the past hurts you have encountered is therapeutic and empowering. But if you take it too far, if you attempt to wipe those hurts from your memory, you could be opening yourself up to harmful people and situations. The best way to keep you moving forward in a healthy, controlled way while keeping those detrimental people and circumstances at bay is planning for and setting boundaries, but this is much easier said than done. Boundaries are one of the most difficult things in the world to create, especially if you lean toward codependency, lack any boundaries, or have a history of dysfunction in your life like I do, but they are also the most important aspect of self-regulation.

A boundary is a line, a rule you create to separate yourself from a possible negative situation. Most boundaries are drawn with a single word: no! Other boundaries can be trickier—it takes a series of choices to take back control of a situation you're in, but once you've done so, you find that the line drawn becomes stronger and easier to stand by every time the situation occurs.

The best place to build a boundary is between yourself and someone with whom you have a toxic relationship. You might not think you have any toxic relationships—and you might not—but take a close look at your interactions. Are there people in your life who leave you feeling physically and emotionally drained, anxious, angry, sad, or even ill? Are there times when, after encountering someone, you lash out at other people? These are all signs of having a toxic relationship. Toxic encounters don't have to be physically or even blatantly emotionally harmful; if you're interacting with someone then drawing into yourself and finding that you need a lot of recovery time for self-care, the initial interaction has to go. That person is having a toxic influence on your life.

I like to call these people *emotional vampires*. They suck all the joy, energy, and positivity out of the room, pick fights, and try to lower your self-esteem. They almost never do it on purpose—most likely they aren't even aware they're being negative or mean—they just have negative voices in their heads all the time and can't break free from their own insecurities enough to be positive and open with another person.

If you find yourself interacting with an emotional vampire, the situation has to go—but that doesn't mean the person has to go. It just means boundaries must be set when it comes to interactions. For instance, if you have a friend who only complains or gossips when the two of you spend time together, place a boundary by only spending time together in groups. That way, when complaining and gossiping gets to be too much, you can make a smooth exit.

Or let's say you find that a friend or acquaintance with whom you've always had a healthy relationship is suddenly wearing you down. Place a boundary by focusing your time together strictly on what might be bothering your friend and causing their negativity. This is a positive boundary, one that will help your friend while also keeping him or her from focusing negativity on you.

Because of our childhood, my siblings and I have all struggled with mental illness, depression, anxiety, or addiction at one point or another. We have been triggers for one another, and it hasn't always been healthy for us to be near one another. At points in our lives when we would get together, we would fall back into old patterns and chaos would take over. I learned that it was easier to meet one-on-one, or not at all, rather than put ourselves in a situation that could quickly turn from a happy gathering to an all-out drunken fight.

A few years ago, I was speaking with one of my brothers and mentioned that it would be nice for all of us to connect regularly at a time other than a wedding or funeral. But for that to happen, there would need to be boundaries in place to stop an argument or fight from breaking out.

Historically, family get-togethers have involved us siblings, our significant others and kids, and a lot of alcohol.

Tension would start to build almost immediately when one person dominated conversation or had one drink too many or the kids were a bit out of hand. Now the four of us in Minnesota meet for breakfast at a local diner once a month for an hour. There's no drinking, spouses, kids, or chaos. We have a timer, and each of us gets fifteen minutes to share stories and catch everyone up on what is going on in our lives. We avoid topics like politics, religion, and our past. We don't necessarily keep it light, but we keep it positive. This might sound extreme to some of you, but it's the only way it works for us.

I love this time we have together. It keeps us connected, and the boundaries make sure that we each are built up by the encounter rather than broken down. It might seem strange to have to set such parameters with family, but there is no magical relationship equation that works for every family. It's okay to take a good hard look at relationships, be they familial, friendly, or romantic, and decide what sort of measures—strange as they might seem—will raise that relationship to the peak of its potential.

So try it now. Think on the relationships in your life and decide what kind of beneficial boundaries could be set.

Ask yourself:
- When would I benefit from setting boundaries?
- What relationships would I improve by setting boundaries?
- What boundaries would make me feel better in _____ situation?

Also remember that how you behave affects how the people around you act. If you are kind and attentive, the people around you will work as buffers and help protect you from emotional vampires.

I've been working with a trainer since my second Snap Fitness opened, and I love having him as a part of the team because he's so open and kind. One day, I was teasing him a little bit (he's from a big family, so I know he could take it) and some of the ladies from his class heard and actually got mad at me. They told me off and told me to leave him alone.

I responded quickly, saying that I loved him too, and that I was just teasing him—I wouldn't have him working with me if he wasn't great! Afterwards, when they were gone, I began to think: *What was so great about him? What was different about him that caused these women to go to bat for him in the face of a threat?* I asked him why, and he jokingly responded that they were only women fighting over a handsome man.

I rolled my eyes. He was younger than me, yes, cuter than me, yes, and in *way* better shape than me, yes—but there were plenty of handsome men around, so that couldn't actually be it, could it? Were his looks truly enough to get them to respond so strongly? I mean, they baked for him, sewed for him, and even invited him on vacation! They acted as his mama bears, taking care of him and defending his name with such loyalty.

So I started to really pay attention, and while he was definitely handsome, it wasn't his looks that were catching clients' eyes. It was how he treated them. He looked them in the eye, called them by name, and poured positive encouragement into them. He never stopped telling them he believed in them and that they were more than capable of achieving their goals. When clients would start to lag with exhaustion, he would touch their arm and tell them that they had three more push-ups in them, and he knew they could do it, even if they didn't know it themselves. He was authentic, compassionate, supportive, sincere, and intentional with each word and movement. He cared deeply about his clients and showed it, and in return, they cared right back, enough to act as his protectors.

While I wouldn't classify myself as an emotional vampire when I teased this trainer, you can see the parallel—I was being perceived as a toxic boss. Because that trainer was so positive and authentic, his clients were loyal enough to safeguard him from what they perceived to be a threat. This buddying-up is a mutually beneficial tactic that can be used casually in a large group. Be the light of the party, make people feel welcome, and they'll repel negativity for you. If there is someone who always seems to control the situation when you meet with him or her, asking a loyal friend to accompany you and be your buffer could help to even out the scale until you're able to manage these encounters on your own.

Calling someone by their name and making eye contact are so needed and often overlooked, especially in the workplace. When was the last time you looked someone in the eyes, gently touched their arm, or poured positivity into them? Who could you offer that to today?

> "THE MOST COMMON WAY PEOPLE GIVE UP
> THEIR POWER IS BY THINKING THEY
> DON'T HAVE ANY."
> —ALICE WALKER

Keeping that control is key. You know what you need in order to be healthy, and you need to position yourself in such a way that you can obtain what you need. If you can't control the situation itself, control everything around the unhealthy event. If you have to meet with a sibling or parent who tears you down, either bring along your buffer or make plans with a friend who always builds you up directly afterwards. If you need to give yourself a way out, plan an appointment, workout class, or another meeting to bookend your encounter and allot a specific amount of time you have available to spend.

Don't judge yourself for needing structure or support. Keeping yourself healthy should be your number one concern. Feel free to let a relationship fade if you're not getting anything positive out of it. If someone is hurting you or is being abusive and you can't maintain the relationship, end it and don't look back. You can't change the world, but you can change your surroundings, and that includes cutting out the people who cut you down.

Saying no to someone or to a situation can be scary, but it's an important part of learning to control potentially toxic situations. If you're afraid that someone might become violent or bait you into a fight, say no over the phone or in the presence of other people. If the reason you're saying no is because you don't like the sound of the situation, try offering another option. If someone wants to go to a place where there will be alcohol and you don't want to do that, say, "How about we take a walk instead?" or, "There's an exhibit at the art museum

I've been meaning to go see—would you like to go there instead?"

Remember that you're the one in control, and that feeling obligated to do something is not the same as having to do it. You have the power to meet on your own terms and a responsibility to yourself to keep situations as healthy as possible. Keep in mind, too, that we only have so many hours in the day. Chances are, you could be doing something valuable—volunteering, spending time with family, taking on a new project— with the time you're currently spending in situations that you wish you could avoid.

As a Minnesotan, it can be hard for me to put myself first and even harder to say no. One way I make this easier for myself is by using a boundary checklist. This helps me catalog my interactions and the steps I need to take to make each one as pleasant as possible. There are times when the boundaries necessary outweigh any potential good, and it becomes much easier for me to say no to someone when all the reasons for it are written out in front of me.

When you're considering setting boundaries for inter-actions with someone in your life, ask yourself these questions:

- Does this person add positivity to my life?
- Is having a relationship with them worth it? Will I be happier if I'm not connected with them? Will I regret it?
- Do I feel better or worse about myself after spending time with them?
- How much time do I feel comfortable spending with them?
- Do I feel better when I visit them alone or with others?
- Do I feel healthier when we meet in public or in private?
- What topics should I avoid discussing with this person?
- Does consuming alcohol make spending time with this person harder?
- How often do I feel comfortable seeing this person?
- Do I need to line up someone to keep me accountable or support me when I spend time with this person?
- What steps do I need to take to stay physically healthy around this person? (For example, meeting outside if they smoke.)

- Who can I talk to if our visit leaves me feeling down?
- How much recovery time do I usually need after I meet with this person?
- What kind of recovery helps me if I'm feeling bad about the visit?

"REMEMBER NO ONE CAN MAKE YOU FEEL
INFERIOR WITHOUT YOUR CONSENT."
—ELEANOR ROOSEVELT

STEP 7

Be Authentic

A year ago, I was visiting someone I care about. Our relationship isn't the healthiest, as she is a glass-half-empty sort of person and we have a long history that includes times when neither of us were at our best. When I was visiting, she was feeling angry and frustrated for whatever reason. She walked up to me, into my personal bubble, looked me in the eye, pointed a finger in my face, and said, "Just so you know, *no one* thinks you're as great as *you* think you are!"

I was shocked and hurt, but I painted on a smile to keep moving forward to get through the day. After I left, I went home, sat in my bed, and cried, and as I did so, I wondered, *Am I great? Do I think I am great? Do others think I am great? What does it mean to be great?* I was suddenly caught up in a cycle of insecurity and low self-esteem, feeling like less than nothing.

When I speak, I often ask the audience to raise their hands if they think they're great. Very few people, if any, raise their hands. When I ask why no one thinks they're great, they say they don't want to seem arrogant, to brag, to show off. My next question is always, "What is the difference between confidence and arrogance?" Lots of people think they are the same, but they're not.

The difference to me between confidence and arrogance is knowing what I am good at and holding my head high to speak clearly about what I do well, but never saying I am better than others. Arrogance is when we think we are the best and brag about being better. It comes from a place of insecurity, thinking that someone being good and happy will in some way take away from your own greatness. Confidence, on the other hand, is being able to find your strengths, gifts, talents, and abilities and walking through life knowing just how worthy you are. It doesn't come from a place of comparison or trying to drag anyone else down. Confident people know that everyone is great at something, even if they don't realize it, and it is because we're all great at different things that the world is a wonderful place!

Confidence is not something that you automatically wake up having; it generally takes years to build up. It can feel like you take giant steps and get nowhere with self-confidence and like your self-confidence crashes with just the smallest incident. Building it back up can seem impossible. But I cannot stress enough to you how important it is to try and do so. Confidence is how you know you're lovable; it's how you find true happiness. And it's key to this step, Being Authentic.

I was wounded for a few days after my half-glass-empty friend told me I wasn't as great as I thought I was, but I did recover. Why? Because I had confidence. Of course my friend's words hurt, but once I looked around at my children and husband who love me, my friends who support me, and my family who has grown so much closer over the years, I realized that I have reasons to think I'm great. I have made strides in my life that I'm truly proud of. I came from a broken place, and now I have the confidence to radiate happiness. I have the confidence to be the happy person who came from a broken place, and that's what makes me authentic.

Being confident means having the strength to be yourself—truly yourself, all of yourself—and that is what authenticity is.

"YOU MAY ENCOUNTER MANY DEFEATS,
BUT YOU MUST NOT BE DEFEATED. IN FACT,
IT MAY BE NECESSARY TO ENCOUNTER
THE DEFEATS, SO YOU CAN KNOW WHO YOU
ARE, WHAT YOU CAN RISE FROM, HOW
YOU CAN STILL COME OUT OF IT."
—MAYA ANGELOU

The first step in gaining confidence is learning to accept the love and encouragement that others offer to you. It can be difficult to embrace, especially if you feel unlovable, but trust them. After all, it's the people around you who will see how exceptional you are, even when you don't. And it isn't only confidence that you could gain. The people who see how amazing you are will want to help you, to boost you up to your potential. You never know when you're going to meet someone who sees something in you and offers a new beginning. This can open some amazing doors for you that might kickstart a life of exceptional living. I know because it happened to me.

When I was seventeen, the *Oprah Winfrey Show* contacted The Bridge for Runaway Youth to find a person who was a great example of becoming an exception. Bill, my mentor and the man who ran The Bridge, offered them my name, thinking I was a good example of a successful teenage runaway (even though I had never technically been a runaway).

I, of course, didn't know about any of this. When the producer for the show called me a few days later, I had been up for almost thirty-six hours partying. I was confused when the phone rang, and when the producer introduced herself, I laughed, said, "Yeah, right," and hung up the phone.

I certainly didn't feel like a success story. I felt beaten down. I was just a teenager renting a small room in a house in Minneapolis. I worked at a temp agency during the day, a coffee shop early in the morning, and a pizza place late at night. I rarely slept, and I was barely getting by paycheck to paycheck.

Fortunately, the woman from *Oprah* called back. She had heard that I was a teenager making it on my own with no parental help and how my tragic and painful childhood had turned out to be a success story. As she was talking, my brain was trying to put it all together, but it didn't click for me as real until she mentioned The Bridge. The phone call was for real, not some joke. As soon as I made that realization, I started to panic. I was afraid that I was going to spoil such an amazing opportunity, so I asked if I could call her back.

Afterwards, I sent all of my friends home and slept for a day and a half. When I woke up, I knew the first thing I needed to do was call Oprah's producer back, but I was hesitant to do so. I was ashamed. Why did I continue to make bad choices? Here was someone who thought I was a success, and I was just coming off a whole lot of bad choices.

When I did work up the courage to call the producer back, she invited me to be a guest on the show. They would fly me and a guest to Chicago and put us up in a hotel. Oprah's limousine would drive us from the airport and to and from the studio. I had never had such luxuries before.

I invited my older sister to join me, and I took in every minute of the trip as only an eighteen-year-old could. When we arrived in Chicago, we were put up in the Knickerbocker Hotel. The producers of the show told us we could order whatever we wanted for room service— not the smartest thing to tell a broke teenager—so of course we ordered everything. I had never before felt so rested, excited, and full. I can remember calling all of my friends from Oprah's limousine phone. *It was a dream.*

My show aired on August 26, 1986—four days before the *Oprah Winfrey Show* went national. The entire experience was incredibly inspiring for me, even though I didn't really feel like the success story everyone kept saying I was. The taping of the show itself was fun, but it forced me to relive some hard memories.

Before I went on air, when I was having my makeup done, I noticed the other two women who were also on the show that day. Both were being fitted with disguises. One had a burn on her neck from her pimp—she was disguised because she was afraid of him finding out she had gone on the show. The other had just gotten out of prostitution and didn't want to be found and pulled back into that world. Being surrounded by these brave, strong women who had it worse off than me, I felt like an imposter. I had struggles, but I also had a safe place to live. I wasn't on the run from anyone, and I didn't have to wear a disguise.

Oprah came and met us before the show. Many people in the audience wanted to know: Is the street really safer than your home? What have you learned trying to take care of yourself? How have you survived? I guess they wanted to understand us, or maybe they wanted us to give them simple answers—but there is nothing simple about abuse, struggling, or living in pain or fear. One of the girls said it is easier to be hurt by a stranger rather than someone you expect to love and protect you.

Some audience members were judgmental and harsh. They told us all to go back home, but they didn't understand we were not wanted there and we were doing the best we could. They couldn't see that the basic resources they took for granted—a loving family, food, and shelter—just aren't things everyone has.

But Oprah was different; she was authentic and kind. She listened to us and told me, "Life is hard. What does not kill you makes you stronger." You see, she also had a challenging childhood, and she overcame much to be where she is today. As we were leaving, she hugged us goodbye and offered additional support to the other two girls, offering a safe place for them to stay while they waited to leave the city. She treated us as equals, not failures. From the way she talked to me, I could tell she believed I was an exception to the rule, that I would not let my past circumstances dictate who I became, and that I would keep growing and improving and would lead a happy life.

I wish today I could go back on the *Oprah Winfrey Show* and show the world that it is possible for someone who was dealt a bad hand in life to achieve success and happiness. In 1986, I wasn't quite there yet. I still had plenty of doubts in myself and what I was capable of accomplishing. But I trusted what Bill from The Bridge saw in me. I allowed him to boost my confidence. And when

Oprah reinforced what he saw in me—that I was an exception to my family's rule of dysfunction and hurt, that I was on my way to making something truly exceptional of my life—that fragile confidence became stronger.

From then on, I was reminded that I was created for more and to listen to the small voice within me saying, "This might be difficult, but so much good will come from it because it will make you stronger and better than you were yesterday." Oprah was such an encourager; she fully believed that no matter what and where we come from, only we determine where we end up. She knew that everyone has the opportunity to live an exceptional life—after all, she has lived it, too.

We don't all have the opportunity to have our confidence boosted by Oprah, but we do all have the opportunity to listen to those around us, those who love us, those who care enough to be honest with us, and trust what they see. Had I never trusted Bill, a man who truly saw me at what I believed to be my worst, I wouldn't be where I am right now. I could have let my own doubts define me, but if I had done so, I would have been living a lie. Because I was never a failure; I was doing the best I could with unfortunate circumstances, but I couldn't see that.

People often say that we shouldn't let others judge our worth, and there is truth to this—don't let toxic relationships bring you down or negative people try to make their truth your own—but there are times when letting someone else's view of you affect your view of yourself is healthy and smart. Listen to your close friends, your loving family, those who you trust. They want the best for you; they'll be honest about what needs to change and what you should be proud of. Let other people help you along in your journey, because once you see what you need to strengthen and what you need to celebrate, you'll be able to be authentic with who you are.

A friend of mine once told me how hard it was for her to get over the negative voices from her childhood. Her parents had yelled at her, called her names, rejected her, and made her feel unloved each day. She told me she felt ugly, like a monster. Even animals were nicer to their babies than her parents ever were to her.

I know it is hard to get over the past—to forgive, to heal, to let go, and to rewrite the tapes. But I told her it was possible because I had seen it. I had done it. But then she told me I was better than her because I forgave my mom and still have a relationship with my mom. But that's not totally true. I am not better. It's just that I have been on a journey for many years, so I have had more time to learn how to heal, forgive, and set healthy boundaries. It isn't always easy, and some days it doesn't work, but I try. It has taken time, and I believe it takes time for everyone, but I've gotten to a point where I'm able to greet each day with a smile and choose to be happy and rewrite the rules.

I was approached once after speaking at U.S. Bank by a man from the audience. He said to me, "I have been watching you for a whole hour, and you have been smiling the whole time. Is your smile real?" I assured him it was and kept smiling. But later, at home, I asked myself: *Is my smile really real? Do I truly feel happiness and joy?* The answer was—and still is—yes. Don't get me wrong, not every day is without struggle or filled with joy; but I am truly happy.

If you have known great sadness, you have the capability to know great joy! I wore a mask with a fake smile throughout my childhood, but today, I wear a real smile, and I try to wear it constantly. I know what it is to love and receive love. I have people around me who support and encourage me to break the cycle, create new traditions, and be the exception. So what's not to smile about?

Being authentic is about putting steps one through six all together. It's about making a conscious decision every day to be worthy of the effort you put into this life. It's about always learning about the people around you and shining positivity into the lives of friends and family and into the world in general.

"BELIEVE IT, BECOME IT,
BE THE EXCEPTION!"
—ANNIE MEEHAN

Everyone is on a different journey; the footprints we leave on their road to happiness are unique to ourselves. Some of us might need every step. Others only need to focus on one or two in the book. Steps might come to us naturally, or they might be the most difficult thing in the world.

I want to honor that exceptional living is different for all of us. Step 7, being authentic and blending together everything that has come before, will mean different things for different people. That is why I invited seven wonderful people to share short essays on how a particular step has contributed to their lives. These seven stories explain each exceptional step from a different perspective. We can all teach each other about parts of every step; these people have taught me how these steps can be applicable in other ways, and I think they can teach you, too.

As you read these, think about where your voice would fit in. What does your exceptional life look like?

Step 1: Be Honest
By Theresa French

Owning my truth came hard and fast in 2010 when I had to admit something. In the matter of just one moment, as I stood in front of a group I was coaching, it hit me in a way I was not prepared for. The truth that I had been avoiding and running from had finally caught up to me.

"Why did you ever quit the photography business?" people would ask. And my answer was always, "Because my family is more important to me than any business." It was a good story . . . but not the whole story, and definitely not the truth.

In 1999, I had the opportunity to pursue the dream of opening my own full-service photography studio. My husband and I left our home in Iowa to move to Minnesota to buy (what would later be revealed to be) a defunct business and several years of heartache.

We arrived in Minnesota without a place to live, without friends or family or any kind of network to rely on. The housing market was booming at this point, and even finding an apartment was impossible, so we moved into the only semblance of a home we could find at the time: the storeroom of the studio building we were trying to buy. A 6' x 8' studio by day, a home by night. There was no shower, only a bathroom with a drain in the floor.

"This is what pursuing bold dreams means," we thought. Until we were informed that the building we were living in and trying to do business in was being repossessed. Within two months, we also learned about the $68,000 Minnesota state tax lien that was soon to be ours if our business transaction was to move forward. On top of that, the bank informed us they would have to seize the building's remaining equipment as a part of the foreclosure.

We were out of options. Yet something in me still drove our dream, to make it happen. By the grace of God, we managed to make a few friends, one of whom allowed us to buy her single-wide mobile home with no money down.

I got to work "making business happen." We found a new building, hung our sign, and in a matter of a short three and a half years, we were able to build a viable, thriving business. By all estimations, we had made it.

It was after midnight on an early fall morning. I was working in my production room, and I heard my husband coming downstairs. When he stood in the doorway of my production room, silent, it was everything I could do to lift my head from what I was working on to ask, "What do you need, honey?"

"It's me or the studio. I want my wife back."

Truth showed up without warning and shook me to my core.

Now it was easy to slip into that, "But I've worked too hard for this, sacrificed too much. How dare you ask me to give it all up? How dare you be so selfish?!" Yet this was the man who left his whole life just three years prior to allow me the opportunity to pursue a dream.

And in that moment, I knew I had to choose between a business that would take my health, my identity, and my marriage if something didn't change. But like so many other times, I delayed any reaction and counted on my ability to always figure it out later.

I had been working seventeen hours a day and seven days a week, which is rarely a symptom of a well-run business. It is a desperate attempt to rob Peter to pay Paul. It was a Thursday when the men in brown arrived at my door with a package marked "Cash COD only." And when I couldn't pay, when I had to admit that I had no money to operate, I had to tell him to come back next week and watch him walk out my studio door with my box and my dignity.

What followed the hanging of the "out of business" sign was a year of becoming a shut-in in my own home, trying desperately to finish the weddings I had signed up already but didn't have money to pay for. I refused to leave my house for fear of being seen.

For eleven months and twenty-two days, I barely got out of bed. I didn't talk on the phone. I didn't answer emails. Yet once again, truth showed up in the form of a voice, one I would unmistakably recognize as God, that said, "I made you for more than this. Now get up and get to work!"

And one day, as I was lying in bed, I began to think about why so many times before I was able to push through, keep moving. And it was in that moment I realized I had lost all value in myself, and I decided that, no matter how I felt, I would take a shower at least once a week, on Tuesdays.

As each Tuesday passed, and each shower appointment was successfully completed, I started feeling myself again. But it took over five years to tell myself the truth, standing in front of a crowd of people who looked to me to be an expert in business and living. Those words were painful but allowed me to see for the very first time that my mistakes were not my identity.

After that presentation, I made it my goal to seek financial education. I read books on business management. All of the things I didn't know, I studied, and now I have created a successful consulting company from it all, helping businesses avoid the devastation I faced.

I am not what I do. I am who I am, and I have intrinsic value. We are all valuable, in spite of our mistakes and misgivings. We fail, but we are not failures, and alone we are valuable, but together we are priceless.

Let your truth reveal your talents, skills, and abilities. Don't hide behind the lies or fancy stories that save face because when you do, you could be taking away someone else's light that is meant to shine by complementing your call in this world.

Theresa French is an inspirational speaker, self-mastery coach, and entrepreneur. Learn more at www.TheresaTalks.com.

Step 2: Be Open
By Teresa Manning

When I pondered on the words "Be open," many thoughts came to me. First the negative: "I'm not," "I can't be," "It's hard, scary, not safe!" Then I explored what ways I have been open in my life and how it has benefited me and opened my life so much. The words that finally came to me and settled with me were, "Be open to the good."

This has been a hard thing in my life. I was raised with thoughts of: there isn't enough to go around; I'm not deserving; I don't really need or deserve good; when is the next shoe going to drop (or the next bad thing going to happen to me)?

Thankfully, when I made a big move in my life to a new town, I was able to begin making lots of shifts. When I searched for and found a new church community and the amazing people there, there were new thoughts I was exposed to, like "Life is about joy" and "There is abundance and you deserve it." These were not easy things for me to swallow. I can remember putting ten dollars in the church basket and crying, feeling like I couldn't believe it was going to be okay to let go of that money, yet also feeling such a sense of relief that I was going to be blessed and taken care of by God and myself and those around me because I was opening myself up to their kindness and love.

I had been raised poor, told that suffering was good, and there would *never* be enough to go around. To think that there *was* enough and that God would take care of me brought a sense of confusion, but so much relief once I was able to fully accept it.

I have begun to be more open to the ideas that life is good, joyful, abundant, and that I deserve that. I can give and accept help and love freely from God and the people around me. How freeing this openness to good has been! Be open to your good!

Teresa Manning is Annie Meehan's older sister and a juvenile probation officer/supervisor in Prescott, Arizona. She has a passion for working with teens and families.

Step 3: Be Healthy
By Val Schonberg

The word "health" means different things to different people. In fact, it's taken on new meaning to me over the years. I was brought up to value health, but most of what I understood about "being healthy" was related to physical health. And, most notably, if you weren't thin, you weren't healthy.

So I pursued thinness. Right along with the rest of our culture, I pursued the belief that if you have the "right" body size and eat the "right" way, your problems will be solved and you will live happily *and healthfully* ever after. And, being a perfectionist, I'm quite certain I did it the "right" way. Unfortunately, there was no "happy and healthy" for me during this time. Now, there's nothing wrong with trying to eat well and stay physically fit. However, when this is your number-one priority in life, there's nothing healthy about it.

Although I struggled with my distorted beliefs about health early on in life, I went on to pursue a master's degree in nutrition science and completed the requirements to be a registered dietitian. I'm fascinated by science and really do love food and eating. So, in many ways, my education was an important part of correcting some of my misunderstanding about physical health. With some practice, my personal relationship with food, eating, exercise, and weight began to come into balance.

The quest for finding peace with food, eating, and weight, however, has less to do with what I eat or how much I exercise than with my lifestyle and learning to manage adversity. Most people know that optimal health is the result of both physical and mental health. But over and over again, people try to quantify this by referencing BMI (body mass index) charts, calorie intake (or calories burned), and even using blood tests to measure stress hormones. What keeps one person functioning when stress, trauma, and pain strike, while another falls to pieces? Resilience. Plenty of research has demonstrated that nutrition and activity are important, but faith, sleep, positive relationships, and stress management all play an important role in overcoming hardship and staying well.

My personal experience of overcoming abuse, divorce, loneliness, and stress, along with my professional experience as a clinical dietitian working in mental health, has clearly demonstrated to me that "being healthy" is more than a person's body size.

Today, I balance my time by living what I teach—eating intuitively and staying active. My priorities are faith and family. My greatest joy is my kids, and cooking, family meals, and quality time with friends and family are a part of my everyday life.

Val Schonberg MS, RD, CSSD, LD, NCM is a dietician, speaker, and teacher. She owns EnlightenU Nutrition Consulting, LLC. Learn more at www.enlightenUnutrition.com.

Step 4: Be Flexible
By Kat Fuoss

My childhood consisted of loving parents and three younger sisters. At the time, I thought everything was normal, and we were just like every other family. It wasn't until my adulthood that I was told my reactions were normal in what was an abnormal environment. I had no idea how this affected me and my relationships until I sought counseling.

It was my normal to see my father pull the phone off the wall (yes, we had a landline phone that was actually on the wall) because he was angry. I saw storm doors leave the hinges and fly into the front lawn. In his anger he would pick up wooden chairs and slam them down so hard, the legs would go flying. On top of all of this was his LOUD voice swearing and ranting on about something that didn't go his way. I remember my sister and I crouching down and taking cover behind the sofa or in a corner behind a plush chair when we heard THAT voice.

We owned a bowling alley, bar, and restaurant, and my sister and I worked there. When a lane would break down (and that happened quite often), all I can remember is anger and rage. My father would kick lockers, the bowling ball returns, and anything in his way on his way to the back of the bowling alley. I remember being scared, bewildered, and embarrassed by his LOUD voice.

Raspberry picking in the sandy Wisconsin terrain got our car stuck every year. My dad would start raising his voice and yelling because he could not get the van out of the sand. My sister and I would be in the back crying out of fear.

One time he was mowing and the riding lawn mower broke down. He tried fixing it (he is not a handyman by any means) but couldn't. His anger erupted and he literally picked up the rider and rolled it. All the while, his voice carried throughout the block.

Growing up, I went to eight different schools (five were high schools). There were only three types of groups who accepted new kids—the geeks, the athletes, or the stoners. Guess which group accepted me? I experimented with alcohol with my newfound friends, and one time I came home drunk and got sick. My father never laid a hand on me in anger, but that night he was so angry he screamed at me and forced my head into the garbage can full of my vomit.

I moved out when I was eighteen, and I discovered that the cycle of anger continued. I would get mad at myself, my friends, my boyfriend, and I would lash out and yell. I remember one time using a cookie sheet as a Frisbee inside my house because I was upset with my spouse over something.

Then I had children, and I vowed to myself to break the cycle. I didn't want my kids growing up in fear. It certainly didn't happen overnight; in fact, my oldest son's last memory of me and his biological dad is me yelling at his father for hiding our checkbook. My son was six.

The decision to want to make a change was my first step. I had to then believe that I was able to transform my behaviors; I had to believe I could be content when things didn't go my way; I had to believe I would become a non-yeller; I had to believe my kids, friends, and family deserved a calm and mature relationship with me; and I had to believe I was capable of breaking the cycle of anger and yelling.

Baby steps—this did not happen all of a sudden. I had to decide to make a conscious choice every time I felt anger bubbling up. Out of counseling, I have come to realize that if anyone raises their voice in anger, it is a real trigger for me. Fear starts to encompass me, but I have learned to put up a "plexiglass wall" and let the words bounce away from me. Today, I am proud to say I do not throw things or raise my voice in anger and am living exceptionally. I believe you can break your cycle!

Kat Fuoss is a documentation specialist at Blue Cross Blue Shield and a virtual assistant. She is an expert in branding and recruiting and was instrumental in the founding of several businesses.

Step 5: Be Gentle
By Diane Windingland

I've come to embrace that famous *Forrest Gump* quote, "Life is like a box of chocolates." For a time, I had resented my life not going as I had planned, just as I used to dislike biting into a chocolate with a coconut center. I've learned to like coconut, just as I have learned to roll with the punches and be happy with whatever life brings my way.

I've discovered three secrets to rolling with the punches: follow your heart, embrace what is, and let go of the past.

Follow your heart—at least some of the time.

Engineering seemed like the logical choice when I was picking a college major. I was good at math and science, and engineering paid well. The only problem was that my first job out of college, designing cruise missiles for a large defense contractor, sucked the life right out of me. One day as I sat at my drafting desk, I popped my head up and looked at the rat-maze of cubicles around me—cubicles filled with tired old men, old enough to be my father, and a few younger men, already with the hunched shoulders and pinched faces of frustrated ambition—and I thought, "Is this all there is?

Is this my future?"

Logically, it was. It was what I trained for. It paid well. But my heart said, "No." Actually, it was more like, "Hell, no!" In fact, I recall telling my husband that I got more joy out of cleaning a toilet. It took a couple of years, but I finally quit and, aside from some part-time jobs now and then, I never have worked for someone else. Sure, I might have made more money if I had stuck it out in engineering, but at what cost? A fractured personality? Years of unhappiness? The pinched face of frustrated ambition?

I'm glad I decided to change my plans. To give myself permission to redefine who I was.

Follow your heart.

Follow your heart and embrace what is. Embrace the present as a gift, even when you have to accept the blessings of an alternate path.

In 1981, at the age of twenty-seven, just nine days after giving birth to my first child, a baby boy, I was rushed to the hospital with severe hemorrhaging. Later that day, after four hours of surgery and ten units of blood, I discovered that my first child would be my last. To save my life the doctor had performed an emergency hysterectomy.

That wasn't what I had planned. And I had to

mourn the loss in order to embrace a new reality. I would never again feel the flutter of new life growing inside me. I would never give birth to another child. I would never have a mini-me, a baby girl who looked like me. I regretted what I would never have.

Three years after that we adopted a baby girl, a beautiful blond-haired, blue-eyed little girl who looked nothing like me. She didn't grow under my heart, but she grew in my heart.

It wasn't what I planned. It was an alternate path to parenthood. It was a blessing of an alternate path. Find the blessings and embrace what is.

It shouldn't come as any surprise that you can't change the past. Why stew over something you can't change? You can't change the past. Whenever you start feeling a twinge of regret, say these five words: I can't change the past. Try it now. Say it like you believe it.

"I can't change the past." Those were the words I told myself as I opened the door to my kitchen pantry and looked at the pencil marks that measured my children's growth. I ran my finger over the lines, read the names and the dates, and smiled as I saw how my youngest son, Yuri, whom we adopted at age twelve from Russia, had been so much shorter than his sister, but within three years was six inches taller. And then, with a wistful pain, I closed the door, wondering for a moment if I could take it off its hinges and keep it forever. I had thought I would be living in that home forever; but no. We lost that home in a foreclosure in 2011. And it was time to go. Time to let go of the past. Time to not be bitter about what I couldn't change, but to move on and be a better person, a more compassionate person, a more grateful person. I simply had to let go of the past.

So, I took a last look around, walked out of the house and into my car, glanced in my rearview mirror, and never looked back.

It's hard to go forward if you are living life looking at the rearview mirror.

When you catch yourself in a moment of regret, looking to the painful past, say, "I can't change the past." And replace the thought of "I wish I had" with "Next time, I will . . ."

You can't change the past, but you can affect the present and the future. So when it comes to the past . . . let it go.

When you are at the crossroads of heart and mind, follow your heart. If things don't turn out as you planned—and they usually don't—accept the blessings of an alternate path. Embrace what is, and then let go of the past.

Diane Windingland is an author, speaker, coach, and communication expert. She is the founder of Small Talk, Big Results. Learn more at www. SmallTalkBigResults.com.

Step 6: Be Courageous
By Karen L. Amundson

During my time as a high school Sunday school teacher, I often told my students being scared wasn't an excuse to not do something. I have carried my own advice with me throughout the years, whether it be when I am at a job interview, crossing a steep mountain pass with a scary dropoff on both sides, or some other endeavor where I feel scared and unsure of myself. I am a firm believer that having courage doesn't mean you never experience fear. To me, courage means you move forward anyway and don't let those negative feelings stop you.

I have gone through more of those scary experiences this past year than I think I ever have.

I've found that I am getting more sensitive and am more in tune to my feelings as I get older. I lost one job and, luckily, was able to find another right away. However, the second job was making me incredibly ill, as it was so high-stress. But in less than six months, I lost that one as well. Afterwards, I was one of the happiest people you could ever wish to meet.

I decided I wanted to feel like that all the time, so I made two huge, scary decisions within a very short time span. The first was a decision to hike the Superior Hiking Trail. I still can't believe I had the courage to spend twenty-seven days alone in the wilderness! I backpacked a total of 270 miles from Canada to Duluth.

At times, I went for hours—and sometimes well over a day—without seeing another person. The Internet and phone connectivity on my trip was often nonexistent. I was completely cut off from all support and human contact and was extremely vulnerable. It was during those times that I had to evolve from relying on the support and positive influence of others to believing and trusting one hundred percent in myself. It gave me plenty of time to think about where I wanted to go and who I wanted to become.

My second decision was, in some ways, scarier than the first. It was the pursuit of a lifelong dream: owning my own business. That led me to launching KLA Outdoor Adventures so I could help other people learn about themselves and experience the world the way I did when I was hiking.

I came out of these experiences knowing I am capable of accomplishing so much more than I ever thought possible. I now have an incredible sense of self-worth and self-reliance. That experience taught me the incredible power we all have to be an amazing, positive influence on others and on ourselves. We cannot only reach toward our full potential but we can help others do the same. When I accomplish something that is out of my comfort zone, it gives me the courage to keep going toward bigger and scarier goals. Those experiences build on one another and help me to grow.

Karen L. Amundson is the founder of KLA Outdoor Adventures, a company that provides mentoring, trip planning, and guide services for customized adventures. Learn more at www. KLAOutdoorAdventures.com.

Step 7: Be Authentic
By Janie Jasin

A few years ago, I bought a dear little stuffed bear. It wore a torn sweater, a worn-off glove, and a little scarf. Its face was worn smooth on the right side. Even though it was old and falling apart, I began to use it in my talks as a professional speaker. The little bear looked like it had been so loved that its face, sweater, and paw were all worn off.

Between talks the little bear sat on my prop shelf. Some years later, I was discussing my will with my children.

"What do you want?" I asked, thinking that we were going to be talking about dollars, antiques, books, and more. It was then that my youngest son—who was forty-four at the time—said, "I want that bear that looks like he was so loved that his fur has worn off."

To my son, that bear was real. It was authentic and genuine. It had lived, and everyone knew it. To be real and genuine, we struggle through storms, pain, and loss.

We all seek to be accepted as we are, with all

of our defects.

But the journey of having our paw worn, our sweater ripped, and our faces void of makeup or phoniness is rough, and it damages us.

I never accepted my worth until someone else saw it. I was blind to it. Forty-five years ago, a woman said to me with conviction, "You hold such promise." These were words I never heard before, and I treasured her words and began to believe them. With all of my defects, losses, talents, beliefs, and love, I listened.

What does it take to know your authentic self, to make your presence genuine, to be real, to show love, sorrow, kindness, and caring?

To be authentic is to allow the bravest part of you to own up to your defects and be grateful for your assets. To love your torn sweater. To embrace a cheek scarred from too many touches. And to recognize the value in other people as worn as you are.

Janie Jasin is an award-winning speaker and best-selling author of The Littlest Christmas Tree. *Learn more at www.janiespeaks.com.*

"SPREAD LOVE EVERYWHERE YOU GO. LET
NO ONE EVER COME TO YOU
WITHOUT LEAVING HAPPIER."
—MOTHER TERESA

Being authentic and loving your life is not about being one hundred percent happy with your life one hundred percent of the time. It's about loving the people in it—even the ones who aren't perfect—however you can. It's about practicing these steps every day and leaving a crack in the doorway to save space for those who want to join you in leaving the past and negativity behind. Speak truth to yourself. Decide to stay empowered even when life is hard. You may take one step forward and then take two back, but the next time you might take two steps forward and only one back.

These steps are meant as a guide to use over and over all through your life. The truth really can set you free; it might be painful, but only after you have come to terms with the realities of yourself and your situation can you take steps toward betterment. Remember that we all do the best we can in our moments of reaction. Our best might not be good enough for those we love or even for ourselves, but we can always go back and make amends, and we can always go forward and do it differently the next time.

It is when we choose to change that we see the results we desire. There are still days, even weeks, that those feelings of abandonment and worthlessness placed upon me by my mom and dad return to me. But I make a conscious effort to remember that my mother loved me as best she could, and that my father's abuse does not define me, and the time I stay wrapped within that negativity is a bit shorter each time.

I no longer beat myself up for being overly sensitive at times. I just am what I am. I have gone to counseling for many years on and off, and it always gives me a new perspective on my life. I will go back as needed throughout my life. I also spend a lot less time around negative people. I now go to bed embracing that I'm imperfect and in peace with that imperfection rather than laying awake frustrated that not everything in my life is perfect. I thank God I only messed up three things today instead of ten and am freed from the need to get it all right.

Be on your journey, and allow these steps to help guide you. In the right time, healing will come. Wounds can be deep, but you can be healed. Like you, I just want to live free, be happy, and, more than anything, be a hero to my kids. I want them to know they are loved, they are valued, and that I am here for them. I never received that, so I know how valuable those affections are, and I consider it a gift to be able to give that affection to them.

Glow for others. Bring happiness and light into the room, and inspire positivity. Be the best version of yourself, but when you can't live up to your own expectations, be kind and gentle with yourself—you are good and you deserve good in your life, even if it takes time to achieve your goals. Surprise people with kindness, and be more and better than what you receive.

Be the living exception—the one that breaks the rules. Instead of lowering your standards to what your circumstances have told you that you deserve, go above the status quo and raise your standards and your belief in what you can accomplish! If you are happy and energetic, the world around you will notice and respond to it. You will be happier each day as the world rises up to meet you.

Walk this journey with me so we can share our smiles with this hurting world. **Let's join together and BE THE EXCEPTION!**

Acknowledgments

Thank you to God for blessing me, having good plans for me, sending angels often to rescue me, sending his Holy Spirit to guide me to forgive and heal, for always being there to whisper in my ear, "Keep the faith, and keep moving forward," and especially for being the one Father who would never harm me.

I want to thank my husband, Greg, for always believing in me and for encouraging me on this challenging journey of sharing my story and my secrets so I can live more fully in freedom and joy and encourage others on their journey.

I want to thank my three children for always giving me love and support, even on my crabby days. I appreciate all the times they've told me I'm a good mom, even when I don't feel like one, and for saying, "Mom, it doesn't matter what others say, we know what an amazing lady and mother you are."

Thanks to Kat Fuoss, my first assistant, who pushed and believed in me to become all I was created to be. And to Nancy, Connie, and Diane, who helped me write what was the first version of this book. Also to my siblings who took time to read part of my story and continue to push me to keep writing and to publish my book. Your support means the world to me.

I would also like to thank the Wise Ink team for helping me shape my book into something exceptional. Laura Zats, Savannah Brooks, and Patrick Maloney made my words sound beautiful, Kim Morehead made them look beautiful, and Theresa French, my wonderful friend, gave me a cover that reflects who I am.

Thank you also to Nancy Lee Guache, Joe Schmit, Don Shelby, and all the wonderful people who contributed to this book and the launch. I couldn't have done this without you.

I want to thank all the women of Women of Words (WOW) for sharing their lives and taking time to read and give me feedback on this journey. Without all of your love, support, and encouragement, this book would still be in piles or stuck inside of my mind. Thank you for everything.

Finally, I want to thank all the friends and family who have supported me along this journey—members of Bible studies, Mastermind groups, my advisory board, the National Speakers Association, neighbors, and so many more encouragers. You supported and believed in me and my ability long before *I knew enough to believe in myself.*

Support and Resources

- **Alcoholics Anonymous:** Find a meeting in your area.
  Website: www.aa.org
- **The Bridge for Youth:** 1111 West 22nd Street, Minneapolis, MN 55405.
  Phone: 612-377-8800
  Website: www.bridgeforyouth.org
- **Nami:** The National Alliance on Mental Illness, the nation's largest grassroots mental health organization.
  Website: www.nami.org
- **National Coalition for the Homeless:** A national network focused on ending homelessness and supporting those currently experiencing it.
  Phone: 202-462-4822
  Website: www.nationalhomeless.org
- **Narcotics Anonymous:** Support nationwide in the form of meetings.
  Website: www.na.org
- **SAVE:** The National Suicide Prevention Hotline, a non-profit hotline for those in need of emergency mental health support.
  Phone: 1-800-273-8255

- **RAINN:** The Rape, Abuse and Incest National Network.
  Phone: 1-800-656-HOPE
  Website: http://centers.rainn.org
- **The United Way Hotline:** A 24-hour information hotline for health and human services.
  Phone: 211

Recommended Reading

- *7 Habits of Highly Effective People* by Steven Covey
- *20,000 Days and Counting* by Robert D. Smith
- *Battlefield of the Mind* by Joyce Meyers
- The Bible or any faith-based daily devotional
- *Breaking Free* by Beth Moore
- *Dare to be Different* by Sando Forte
- *Getting Kids to Mind Without Losing Your Mind,* and *Sex Begins in the Kitchen* by Kevin Lehman
- *God Calling* edited by A. J. Russel
- *The Magic of Goals* by Ronald Reynolds
- *Monday Morning Choices* by David Cottrel
- *One Great Goal* by Ursula C. Mentjies
- *Overcoming the Nevers* by Teri Johnson
- *The Power of the Praying Wife* Stormie O'Martin
- *The Power of Who* by Bob Beaudine
- *The Red Velvet Dress* by Francine Rivers
- *The Shack* by William Paul Young
- *Simple Abundance: A Daybook of Comfort and Joy* by Sarah Ban Breathnach
- *The Traveler's Gift* by Andy Andrews
- *Unthink* by Erik Wahl

"WE START TO CHANGE WHEN WE MAKE THE CHOICE TO TAKE A CHANCE."
—ANNIE MEEHAN, INTERNATIONAL SPEAKER AND LIFE COACH

Book Annie Meehan

"Annie is a tremendous speaker. She balances her presentation with positive stories. Her message regarding the Oprah Show is priceless. People want to know how all the stories end. That's a sign that she connects and people relate well to her—they wonder!"

—Patricia A. Johnson, VP Finance Operations, Target

"Anyone who believes you have to die where you were born needs to meet Annie. Her story inspires you to move out of your circumstance and be better. She is a living example of how we can transform with determination, faith, and a little help from others."

—Jearlyn Steele, WCCO Radio

"Annie is a very dynamic and energetic speaker. Her charisma captures your heart and makes you delve deep into yourself and look beyond the basics."

—Judy Peterson, Peterson Travel Pros LLC

To get on Annie's calendar, call
952-994-8356 or email Annie
at **annie@anniemeehan.com**.